FREEZER
HINTS

FREEZER
HINTS

Random Little Library
an imprint of
Random House Australia Pty Ltd
20 Alfred Street, Milsons Point NSW 2061

Sydney   New York   Toronto
London   Auckland
and agencies throughout the world

Series Co-ordination: Gordon Cheers
Design: Liz Nicholson, Design Bite
Typeset by Axiom, 139 Charles Street, Abbotsford Vic 3067
Production by Vantage Graphics, Sydney
Printed by Australian Print Group, Maryborough

ISBN 0 09 182806 6

CONTENTS

—— 1 ——

Freezer basics 1

—— 2 ——

Packaging 27

—— 3 ——

*Defrosting and
reheating 43*

—— 4 ——

*Soups, sauces
and cereals 59*

—— 5 ——

Meat 69

—— 6 ——

Fish and poultry 83

—— 7 ——

Vegetables 101

—— 8 ——

Fruit 125

—— 9 ——

*Desserts and
baking 151*

—— 10 ——

*Dairy products
and eggs 177*

FREEZER
BASICS

Freezing is a quick method of safely preserving food. The advantages of home freezing and bulk buying can be appreciated by anyone who enjoys cutting costs and time-wasting chores and varying and improving their family's diet. Although food is not improved by time spent in the freezer, provided the food put in is correctly processed, packed and thawed and not stored longer than the recommended time, then it will taste just as good as it did when it went in.

If you are going to invest money in a freezer, then pay a larger electricity bill, and devote your time and energy to proper packaging and so forth, it makes sense to only use the best quality produce. Freezing never improves the quality of inferior food.

Even the small freezer compartment in a refrigerator can be a great advantage. You can make a casserole, eat some and freeze some, instead of eating it several nights running. Or you can take out a prepared meal and quickly reheat it in the microwave oven when you have been working late and want a meal quickly.

This first chapter introduces the freezer and how to use it. However, it is not a substitute for reading the manufacturer's handbook that goes with your model, which you should read to familiarise yourself with your own freezer.

Air space
Your freezer must be surrounded by 3 cm air space on either side, 11 cm behind it and 9 cm above it in order to operate properly.

Baby food
Puréed, cooked foods such as meat, vegetables and fruit can be successfully frozen for use as baby food.

Cook food that is to be frozen and leave it to cool completely. Place in a blender and blend until smooth. Divide into small portions and pack in rigid containers, leaving a 2 cm headspace, or in plastic bags, expelling as much air as possible. Only freeze as much as is needed for one meal.

Blanching
Blanching is an excellent way of preserving the colour and texture of vegetables or fruits which

normally discolour when frozen raw, and eliminates the need for sugar or sugar syrup.

Wash and halve or quarter the vegetables or fruit and remove stones or seeds, then either steam blanch or water blanch.

A minute timer is extremely useful, as over-blanching can often cause young tender vegetables to cook completely and they will not keep their flavour as well once cooked and frozen.

Not blanching for long enough can cause loss of nutritional value and 'off' flavours to develop in some vegetables.

When plunging the vegetables into cold water, keep the cooling water as cold as possible.

See also Steam blanching, Water blanching

Blanching in the microwave

Fruit and vegetables can be blanched very successfully in the microwave and in much smaller amounts of water than usual.

Small quantities blanch more evenly than large — if necessary blanch in batches, microwaving the first batch while preparing the next batch.

A 2 litre casserole is suitable for most fruit and vegetables.

Bulk buying and cooking

Arrange to have bulk purchases of meat delivered or collect it ready frozen and packaged in heavy-duty plastic bags. It is easier for the butcher to freeze meat than it is for you.

You can further divide up the butcher's packs into meal-sized portions at home. Never leave meat in such large packs that you have to partially defrost it, divide and refreeze some of it.

Never buy food in bulk just because it is cheap. Cheaper food is usually of poorer quality. Also, there is little point in buying in bulk if the food will not be eaten within its storage life.

When buying in bulk, make sure there is enough room in the freezer to store the purchased food. A lot can depend on the packaging and the shape of the food packages stored. Choose foods that your family likes and will eat in quantity, and balance the quantities and types of food to be stored.

Freezing is the only way of safely preserving cooked dishes. Organise the cooking ahead so that two or three meals are always ready in the freezer.

Convert raw materials such as bulk-bought meat into cooked dishes as soon as they have been bought to save storage space.

Double or treble quantities of dishes such as casseroles, using one immediately and saving the other portions for future use with added seasonings. Batch cooking will also take full advantage of oven heat.

Candles
To make candles burn more slowly, freeze them for several hours before lighting.

Cleaning and care
If your freezer is brand new, wipe around the inside with a cloth or sponge soaked in a solution of bicarbonate of soda (1 teaspoon soda to 1 litre warm water). When the freezer is dry, plug in and wait for at least 2 hours for the temperature to drop before using. Clean the outside of the freezer with warm soapy water.

Never use soap, detergent or caustic cleaners to clean a freezer.

See also Defrosting

Coffee
Ground coffee and coffee beans freeze well and retain their flavour.

Strong brewed coffee can be poured into ice cube trays and later used for iced coffee. It will keep for 3 months in the freezer.

Cooking for the freezer

When preparing a dish for the freezer, season it lightly.

Synthetic vanilla essence, cloves and pepper all become bitter during freezing. Add these flavourings later.

Use shallow rather than deep dishes.

Cool everything as rapidly as possible and freeze at once.

Hard-boiled eggs are best added after removing a cooked dish from the freezer. Frozen hard-boiled eggs tend to have a rubbery texture when defrosted.

Rice salads become grainy after defrosting and are best cooked as required.

Jam and golden syrup do not freeze well by themselves and, therefore, this should be kept in mind when planning to freeze dishes like hot steamed puddings.

Always remove surplus fats from food before freezing.

Cooking from frozen *see* chapter 3, 'Defrosting and reheating'

Cooling

If food that is to be frozen has been cooked or blanched, make sure that it is cooled rapidly and thoroughly by first placing it in the refrigerator.

Never put anything warm or hot into a freezer.

Cross-flavouring

Some highly flavoured or highly seasoned foods can transfer their flavour to others. The main culprits are garlic, cheese and onion-flavoured dishes, curries and raw ingredients.

Double-thickness and firmly secured wrappings will prevent cross-flavouring.

Defrosting the freezer

Frost and ice will build up inside your freezer and should be removed regularly when it is about 5 mm thick. Try to defrost when stocks are low, and on a cold day if possible.

In between defrosting keep down the frost and ice by scraping off as much as you can from time to time with a plastic or wooden spatula — never use a metal utensil.

Make sure that there is no ice to prevent the lid or door from closing properly.

A chest-type freezer will need defrosting only one or twice a year; an upright one will need it three or four times a year.

When defrosting, also dust the condenser tubes.

Newspapers or clean old sheets placed in the freezer a few hours before defrosting will provide chilled wrappings for the frozen food.

Help the defrosting by placing bowls of

hot water inside the cabinet.

Never use electrical appliances, such as hair-driers or heaters, in an attempt to help defrost the freezer. You could get an electric shock.

Defrosting the freezer will be easier next time if you spray the internal walls of your newly defrosted freezer with a light oil spray (e.g. Pure and Simple) before turning it back on.

Don't freeze ...

... mayonnaise, egg custard, single, double or unpasteurised cream, milk (except homogenised), and cottage cheese.

These foods do not freeze successfully because they tend to separate and cannot be whisked back to their former state when defrosted.

Other non-starters in the freezing world are cucumbers, lettuce, tomatoes, onions, celery, boiled potatoes, straw-berries, soft meringue toppings and most fried foods.

Never place aerosol cans, volatile or flammable material or carbonated drinks in your freezer as they might explode.

Dry pack

Fruits that discolour easily, such as blackcurrants and raspberries, can be frozen whole without the addition of sugar or syrup.

Spread the fruit on trays and place in the freezer unwrapped until firm. Then tip into plastic bags and seal securely.

The fruit will remain free-flowing and separate, and can consequently be used in small amounts as desired.

See also Sugar pack, Sugar syrup *and* chapter 8, 'Fruit'.

Fast freeze switch

The faster fresh food is frozen, the better its quality will be protected. Because fast freezing results in smaller ice crystals there will be less 'drip' (the liquid lost from defrosting food). The fast freeze switch on your freezer overrides the thermostat so that the motor keeps the temperature below the normal setting and freezes fresh food quickly.

If your freezer has no fast freeze switch, adjust the thermostat to its coldest setting.

If you only want to place small items, such as one loaf and one casserole, in the freezer, it is probably not necessary to use the switch at all. Simply add the food to the freezer.

For a fairly small amount of food, such as four casseroles and several pies, turn on the fast freeze switch for about 2 hours before adding the food to the freezer and leave it on for about 4 hours more until the food is solid.

For a large quantity of food, such as half a side of meat, turn on the fast freeze switch for about 3 hours beforehand to ensure that the freezer really is cold. Put the meat in and leave for a further 12-18 hours until solid. This suggested timing is for a fully loaded freezer. If the freezer were only half full you could use the switch for less time.

Fast freezing times
Bacon, meat, poultry: 2 hours per 500 g

Fish: 2 hours per 500 g

Vegetables and fruit: 1 hour per 500 g

Prepared meals: 2 hours per 500 g

Bread and cakes: 1 hour per 500 g

Pastries: 2 hours per 500 g

Dairy products: 1 hour per 500 g

Liquids: 1 hour per 500 ml

Fish see Ice glazing *and* Open-freezing

Freezer space
Allocation of space in your freezer will be influenced by the needs of your household, but a useful guide is to allow a quarter of the space to store meat; a quarter to store fruit and vegetables; a quarter for home-cooked dishes and semi-prepared dishes such

as uncooked pastry or bread dough; and a quarter for bread, cakes and oddments like sauces or prepared meals.

Freezing

Do not aim to freeze more than a tenth of the freezer's storage capacity — or the amount recommended by the manufacturer — at one time.

Never put warm food in the freezer; it will increase the inside temperature and might possibly defrost frozen food slightly. Cool food quickly and thoroughly before freezing.

In hot weather, food can be chilled in the refrigerator before freezing.

See also Fast freeze switch

Fruit *see* chapter 8, 'Fruit'.

Handling

Always handle food that is to be frozen quickly, because it begins to deteriorate rapidly.

If you are planning to freeze your own produce, or if you have bought directly from the farmer, remember that fruit and vegetables should be frozen within six hours of picking if possible.

All fresh fish should be frozen within 24 hours of being caught, and preferably within 12 hours.

Headspace

Liquid expands by about a tenth of its volume when

frozen as does food with a high water content, such as strawberries. To prevent the container bursting open during freezing, room must be allowed for expansion below the top of the container.

Allow about 1 cm in wide containers, 2 cm per 500 ml liquid in narrow containers, and about 1 cm per 500 g fruit.

If more space than this is left, fill the gap with crumpled foil or grease-proof paper to block out air.

Holidays

When you go away on holiday, you can leave your freezer operating normally.

If your freezer is going to be switched off for a long time, you must empty it, switch it off and unplug it, clean the inside thoroughly and leave the door or lid open (to prevent smells caused by bacterial growth, which are difficult to remove).

Ice glazing

Whole fish freeze best if they are covered with a layer of ice — a method known as ice glazing.

To ice glaze a whole fish, place it in the freezer, unwrapped, until firm. Then remove it from the freezer and dip into cold water until there is a thin film of ice over the fish.

Return it to the freezer until firm once more.

Repeat this process at half-hourly intervals until there is an ice covering 5 mm thick over the fish.

Then wrap the fish in freezer wrap, overwrap in a plastic bag and return it to the freezer.

Insulated containers
Special bags and boxes are available in which frozen purchases can be carried home or frozen food taken on picnics.

Knives
Serrated, sharp knives that saw and slice frozen food are available.

Warming the blade will help to cut through frozen food.

Labelling
Always label and date packets of frozen food clearly.

See chapter 2, 'Packaging'.

Location
Your freezer must not be located in frosty or unprotected areas, such as a verandah.

It must be kept dry, away from excess moisture, steam and humidity, and away from direct sunlight. It must also be located away from direct heat sources, such as stoves, fires or heaters.

If the freezer is in a dark room, make sure there is some kind of lighting available so you can find things at the bottom.

Your freezer needs to stand on a solid, level floor.

Microwave defrosting *see* chapter 3, 'Defrosting and reheating'.

Moving house
Always check with the removal firm whether they will handle the freezer.

It is a good idea to let stocks run low before moving, but keep some food ready because you might need it on moving day.

If the move is expected to be completed in one day,

the food should not suffer as long as the door is kept shut and the freezer is the last item on to the van and the first off it.

Make sure that you have worked out a suitable new site for the freezer and that there is a power point.

If you have to empty the freezer for the move, pack the frozen food in a tea chest with dry ice or in an Esky.

Noise
Some freezer models are noisier than others. Those with fan-assisted condensers make more noise than those with static plate condensers. The skin-type condensers are the quietest.

If the motor seems to be running a great deal, there may be dust on the condenser or it may be time for a defrosting session.

A very noisy compressor could mean that there is something wrong or that the machine is getting old.

Open-freezing

Open-freezing, also called free-flowing freezing, is the term applied to freezing small items on a tray until firm without packaging or covering, then transferring them to a bag or container.

Open-freezing is recommended for berry fruits, sausages, hamburgers, chops, small fish, fish steaks and fillets.

Small fish can be open-frozen either by placing them flat on a tray or by hanging them by their tails inside a storage basket.

Using wooden clothes pegs, peg the fish to the base of a wire-covered storage basket which you have turned upside down, so that the fish hang head down. Then place the basket in the freezer until the fish are firm. Unpeg them and package for freezer storage in the usual way.

For smelly items like onions and cauliflower, place the tray inside a big plastic bag and seal it loosely while open-freezing.

Decorated cakes and tarts should also be open-frozen

before packaging to prevent their icing being damaged by plastic wrapping.

Packaging materials

Use packaging materials that are moisture- and vapour-proof as well as resistant to cross-contamination with other foods. Exposure to air and moisture will damage frozen foods causing them to lose quality. *See* chapter 2, 'Packaging'.

Power cuts

Power cuts are rarely disastrous for frozen foods because they don't often last more than a couple of hours and, provided a few simple rules are followed, food is perfectly safe in the freezer for up to 24 hours.

If you have advance warning of a power cut, move ice cream and cream cakes (if in rigid containers) to the bottom or back and stack more dense items, such as meat, at the top of the freezer.

Fill any gaps with boxes or crumpled newspaper to cut down on air circulation.

Switch on to fast freeze for a couple of hours.

Don't open the door or lid until power is back and the freezer has had time to return to normal temperature.

Dry ice can be used as a last resort to keep food

frozen. It comes in large blocks and needs to be chopped into small pieces. Handle with care, use gloves and keep it well away from your skin.

Place frozen food in a carton or tea chest and place cardboard on top, then tightly packed dry ice. Continue to pack the food in layers like this. It should help for at least 24 hours.

After a 24-hour cut check whether anything has defrosted. Food that has defrosted but is cold or contains ice crystals will probably have lost some quality and good appearance but will still be safe to eat.

Pre-cooked meat, fish and poultry that has defrosted

should be used immediately or discarded.

Food that has completely defrosted and ceases to feel cold should be discarded.

Power supply
Your freezer must be plugged into its own power point. Do not use it in conjunction with extension cords or double adaptors.

Quantities
Freeze foods only in small usable quantities. Left-over defrosted food should never be refrozen.

Refreezing
If you have an extended power cut or breakdown or the power is accidentally switched off and the food in your freezer defrosts,

some food can be refrozen and some cannot.

Food must still be fresh. If it has gone off, throw it out. Don't take risks. The freezer cannot make food fresher or kill bacteria.

When food is defrosted and then refrozen, the cell structure can be damaged, which means that there may be a loss of colour, texture, flavour and nutritional value.

Because of its high water content, fruit collapses, so don't refreeze it in the same form. Instead use it to make purées or syrups.

Raw meat, fish and poultry should never be refrozen. Instead cook it and turn it

into casseroles, pies or roasts, then refreeze.

Fish can be turned into flans, fish cakes or casseroles.

Prepared meals, such as frozen cooked meat or fish dishes, should not be refrozen.

Bread, cakes and pastry can be refrozen, except for cakes containing cream. Bread will be a little staler after refreezing.

Ice cream, cream and synthetic cream, or foods containing them, should never be refrozen.

Once food has been refrozen it should be used up as soon as possible.

Safety precautions

Never lick ice direct from the freezer as it will burn your lips and tongue.

Make sure the freezer is switched off and unplugged at the power point before defrosting, cleaning or moving.

Make sure the power point used for your freezer is earthed; otherwise it might give you an electric shock.

Salt

As salt becomes stronger in taste during freezing, it is best to use less than normal when preparing cooked meat dishes and add more when you reheat them if it is needed.

Salt has the effect of accelerating rancidity in fatty foods stored in the freezer.

Smells

An opened package of bicarbonate of soda left in the freezer will help remove odours caused by placing strong-smelling foods inside. Replace the package with a fresh one every two months.

A smell of food that has gone off may be noticeable from a broken pack of overblanched vegetables or from a fatty food that has been stored for too long and has begun to go rancid.

A more likely cause of smells in the freezer would

be insufficient wrapping of pungent foods such as curries and garlic-flavoured dishes, onions, cheese or cauliflower.

Avoid smells occurring in the freezer by open-freezing the foods at risk and overwrapping them with a large bag.

Spices

The flavour of spices seems to deteriorate after 3-4 months in the freezer so spiced dishes should not be frozen for longer than 2 months.

The flavour of crushed or chopped garlic deteriorates quickly in the freezer and should be added to dishes when they are reheated.

Steam blanching

Use a steamer or a metal colander suspended over a saucepan of boiling water. When the water is boiling rapidly, place up to 500 g prepared vegetables over the steam, cover with a lid and leave in the steam for the recommended time.

(Steam blanching takes 1 minute longer than water blanching.)

Stir the vegetables occasionally to improve the penetration of the steam.

Have ready a bowl of ice-cold water (put lots of ice cubes or a brick of ice in it).

Drain the blanched vegetables and stand in the iced water for the same length of time as they were blanched, stirring occasionally. Drain well.

Spread the vegetables in a single layer on a tray and open-freeze for about 30 minutes or until they have begun to freeze and can be packed into plastic bags.

The chilled water can be used for subsequent batches of vegetables without the addition of more ice cubes and, when all the vegetables have been processed, it can be kept as stock for soup-making.

Sugar pack
The sugar pack method is particularly suitable for berry fruits, but can be used for other fruits if desired. Fruits that

discolour should be immersed in a solution of ¨ teaspoon ascorbic acid, crushed and dissolved in 1 litre cold water for 10 minutes, then removed with a perforated spoon and sprinkled with caster sugar in the ratio of 125 g per 500 g fruit.

See also Dry pack, Syrup pack

Syrup pack
Fruits that tend to discolour easily and firm fruits, such as peaches and pears, are best frozen in a sugar syrup.

The syrup must always be cold and it is possible to make it in advance and keep it in the refrigerator for several days.

Make a syrup by dissolving 250 g sugar in 500 ml water. Allow about 300 ml syrup to every 500 g fruit.

Dip the fruit into lemon juice, then pack into rigid containers and cover the fruit with the syrup, submerging it by placing a piece of crumpled greaseproof paper or foil on top.

Make sure that there is a headspace of about 2 cm before sealing to allow for expansion.

See also Dry pack, Sugar pack

Temperature

Always maintain a steady temperature of –18°C.

Do not open the lid or door too frequently, and do not add too many fresh packets of food at one time without using the fast freeze switch correctly.

Thermostat

When you buy your freezer the thermostat should be set at the correct temperature.

You can make sure that the thermostat is operating correctly by using a freezer thermometer to measure the temperature.

Adjust the thermostat if necessary.

Unused space

Freezers are far more efficient users of energy when they are full.

If your freezer is more empty than it should be, fill with boxes containing crumpled newspapers to cut down on running costs. Stack the boxes in the top section of an upright freezer.

Another idea is to fill gaps with empty milk cartons which have been filled with water and sealed. These also make handy ice bricks to take on picnics.

Vegetables
Vegetables can be frozen in a variety of ways, depending on the kind of vegetable and its eventual use. The majority should be blanched as enzymes, which cause deterioration of the vegetable, even

in the freezer, are only destroyed by high temperatures.

See Steam blanching and Water blanching.

Warning light
If your freezer's warning light comes on, check whether the door is open (which might be due to a build-up of frost holding it slightly open); whether the thermostat is set high enough; and whether the ambient temperature (the temperature of the air around your freezer) is too warm.

Also consult your manufacturer's handbook for information about the warning light on your model.

Water blanching

In a large saucepan bring to the boil just enough water to cover about 500 g prepared vegetables.

When the water is boiling rapidly add the vegetables in a blanching basket if available or in a mesh salad basket.

Blanching time is estimated from the moment the vegetables are placed in the boiling water and not from the time the water returns to the boil.

As soon as blanching is complete, proceed with freezing as described for steam blanching.

Precise timing is essential as overblanching can cause young, tender vegetables to cook completely and they will not keep their flavour as well.

Not blanching for long enough can cause loss of nutritional value and in some vegetables the flavour might deteriorate.

Some vegetables, especially those belonging to the marrow family, keep their texture and flavour better by being cooked before freezing rather than by being blanched. Potatoes are also better cooked than blanched.

PACKAGING

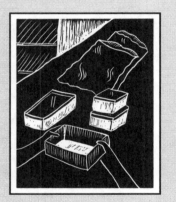

It is essential that food destined for freezer storage be carefully and correctly packaged in the appropriate materials. Packaging materials must be strong, moisture- and vapour-proof, odourless and capable of withstanding very low temperatures successfully. Unless packaging has these features, food will suffer from dehydration and oxidation (also called freezer burn), which will cause discoloration and loss of flavour and nutritional value.

Fortunately there are many packaging products on the market designed specifically for freezers, including cling film, sheet plastic, labels, rigid plastic containers and marker pens. New brands and materials are continually appearing.

If you own a microwave oven as well as a freezer, you should consider whether containers chosen for freezing will also be suitable for microwave defrosting and reheating of the same food. If so, you will be saved a lot of trouble and washing up.

Baskets and dividers

Plastic-covered wire mesh freezer baskets are available for hanging across the top of chest freezers and to use for stacking. Bear in mind that baskets full of food will be heavy to lift.

Dividers can also be used, so that a main division can be made between meat and vegetables or between raw materials and cooked food, for instance.

Butcher's paper

Butcher's paper is not recommended for freezer packaging. It is not moisture- or vapour-proof, and deterioration of the food will result if it is used.

Cake tins

Square or rectangular cake tins can be used to mould foods into regular shape. Line the tin with foil or plastic, freeze the contents and then transfer the solid block to a plastic bag.

Cardboard tubs

Cardboard tubs must have a good-quality wax coating.

Some come with their own lids, others must have lids formed from foil or plastic sheeting and then sealed with masking or freezer tape.

They can be reused with care, but do not wash them in hot water as this will remove the protective wax coating.

Cellophane

Cellophane is not recommended for freezer packaging. It is not moisture- or vapour-proof, and deterioration of the food will result if it is used.

Chinagraph pencil

A chinagraph pencil is a special type of pencil that writes easily on plastic bags and foil and does not come off in the freezer. It is an alternative to a felt-tipped marking pen.

Cling film

Plastic cling film can be used for short-term storage of up to a week. It can be used successfully in conjunction with other packaging material, e.g. individual food items each wrapped in film, then several placed in one large plastic bag or container.

Cling film should be used as a lining before packing acidic fruits in foil and for wrapping individual portions of food which are then stored together in a large plastic bag and removed one at a time.

Flavour transfer

see Smells

Foil

Foil is very useful for wrapping because it can be shaped to cover awkward items and moulded closely around the food to ensure that air does not get in.

Use a single layer of heavy-quality foil or a double

layer if you are using thin kitchen foil.

Seal it by folding the edges closely over each other, if necessary using freezer tape.

Foil should not be used for wrapping acidic fruits, which may react with it. If the foil is likely to be punctured in the freezer, overwrap large items with a plastic bag.

Foil containers

Foil containers come in a variety of shapes and sizes, and are ideal for prepared cooked meals, pies, tarts, etc. Some have their own lids, others need a lid made of sheet foil. They are reusable.

Freezer tape

Freezer tape is a non-cellulose clear sticky tape that withstands freezing temperatures.

Glass

Some glass containers can be used in a freezer.

Test glass containers for freezer suitability by freezing them overnight empty inside a plastic bag. If they shatter, at least the fragments will be caught inside the bag.

Some glass is said to be freezer-safe but even so it is wise to place it inside a plastic bag when in use.

Don't put a cold glass container down on a hot surface.

Always leave headspace in glass containers.

Remember that narrow-necked glass containers such as sauce bottles cannot be used in a freezer.

Items frozen in glass containers must be defrosted slowly in the refrigerator as quick changes in temperature make cracking of the glass more probable.

Glass serving dishes may be placed in the freezer for short-term storage. Thick glass is safer than thin, and the ovenproof type is usually all right if returned to room temperature slowly.

The disadvantage of storing liquids in glass containers is that complete defrosting is necessary and cannot be accelerated by immersing in water or by easing out, as can be done with flexible plastic containers.

Heat sealing
A heat sealer seals plastic bags after filling and is available from electrical appliance shops. A warm domestic iron can also be used for the same purpose.

If sealing plastic freezer bags with your domestic iron, put a piece of brown paper between the iron and the bag.

Ice cream containers
Either plastic or rust-proof tin ice cream containers can

be used in the freezer. Seal the lid with masking tape if it no longer fits snugly.

Ice cube trays

Although ice cube trays are not storage containers, they can be used to form cubes of food which is only required in small quantities, e.g. beaten egg, lemon juice or tomato paste.

They are particularly good for forming meal-sized portions of baby food.

Store the cubes in plastic bags or containers.

Inventory

It is a good idea to keep an inventory of the contents of the freezer in a notebook or on index cards. Write down what you put in the freezer,

the number of packages, position inside the freezer, the date frozen and the date removed.

This is the best way to keep track of the contents of a large freezer but is less important if your freezer is not a big one.

Labelling

Label all food put in the freezer with the name of the food, the date frozen and other useful information, such as whether fruit was frozen with or without sugar.

Label the top of packages and containers if you have a chest freezer; label the side that faces you as you open the door if you have an upright freezer.

Special freezer labels with self-sticking glue which remains attached in freezer temperatures are available from stationers.

These labels can be written on with either waterproof marking pens or ballpoint pens.

Detailed and accurate labelling is absolutely vital. Make sure that every label includes the following information: contents, date frozen, use-by date, thawing time, thawing method, reheating instructions and approximate number of serves.

Freezer labels can also be bought in different colours so that you can use a colour-coding system to identify food in the freezer when you need it.

Anonymous lumps of frozen food really can look identical after a while. You can further help identification by bagging according to type.

All your frozen meat packages, for instance, can be put into a large red string bag. All your vegetable packages can be sealed with green twist ties.

Marking pens

A variety of waterproof marking pens are available. Most can be used to write directly on to plastic bags, plastic containers and foil. Ballpoint pens can be used to write directly on labels.

Masking tape

Masking tape is a wide, buff-coloured, self-sticking tape. It can be written on to label food at the same time as sealing the contents of a container.

Microwave ovens

If you have a microwave oven, you will want to use it in conjunction with your freezer.

Food can be cooked or part-cooked in a microwave, cooled and frozen, then defrosted and reheated in the microwave.

All this can be done in the same container as long as you have used special-purpose cookware that is both microwave-safe and suitable for the freezer.

Cling film cannot be used in a microwave unless it is specifically marked 'microwave safe'.

Foil and foil containers cannot be used in a microwave oven.

Boil-in-the-bag convenience foods and roasting bags (which are ideal for freezing casseroles, vegetables and small joints) can both be put directly into the microwave from the freezer.

Oven bags

Oven bags are especially constructed to withstand oven cooking temperatures, and they also make very strong bags for freezing. They are relatively cheap and can be used for storing food such as chickens, roasting joints, etc, which are intended for cooking in the oven bag later.

Ovenware

Ovenware casserole dishes enable food to be cooked, cooled, frozen then defrosted and reheated in the same dish.

Some containers may crack if reheated straight from the freezer, so defrosting in the refrigerator first is recommended.

Alternatively, line the dish with foil before cooking, then after freezing the solid block of food can be lifted from the container and repackaged in a plastic bag. When reheating, return to the original casserole dish.

Packaging methods

Bad packaging causes a number of problems such as toughness, dryness, lack of flavour and unpleasant mingling of flavours from different foods which, while not rendering the food dangerous to eat, will cause an unattractive appearance.

Packaging food in plastic bags is simple, but remember that expelling air with a vacuum pump is crucial. You could also suck air out with a straw, but a pump would be more efficient and reliable.

Interleaving foods such as steaks, fish fillets and pancakes is necessary to prevent the food sticking together and eliminates the need for defrosting in many instances.

When defrosting is necessary, separated food will defrost more quickly than if frozen as a solid block.

Large plastic bags can be filled with several packages of the same type of food, each package wrapped separately in meal-sized quantities in thin cling film or sheet foil.

Repack large purchases in usable quantities as soon as the food is purchased for freezer storage.

Padding
To prevent puncture and damage to plastic bags in the freezer, pad sharp bones with wads of foil or plastic.

Plastic bags
Plastic bags must be of good quality with strong seams (if any). They are the most versatile of all packaging material and can be used for nearly all types of food. They are reusable with care after washing and drying.

Check used bags to see that no holes or tears have appeared.

Some are labelled 'freezer bags' and these are the best ones to use.

Cheap, catering-size packs of such foods as frozen French fries, fish fingers, ice cream, frozen peas and so on can be repackaged into plastic bags in more usable amounts for good savings of both money and shopping time.

Plastic containers

Plastic containers are good for the storage of liquids and foods with a high liquid content. They must have well-sealing lids and be made of a good-quality flexible plastic.

Containers made from hard plastic frequently become brittle and split at low temperatures.

When packaging food in the container, allow headspace of 1 cm per 500 ml before putting the lid on and freezing. Liquids expand when they are frozen and will push lids off containers if headspace has not been left.

When you're running out of freezer-proof containers for liquids, try this. Line a container with a plastic freezer bag, pour the liquid into the bag, seal and freeze within the confines of the container. Later, remove the bag from the container which you can now use again.

Square shapes make more economical use of space in the freezer than round, as are containers which will stack one on top of another.

Plastic containers of some bought foods are useful in

the freezer (but not in the microwave oven). Examples are butter or margarine tubs and yoghurt containers.

They must be absolutely clean. Use freezer tape to ensure an airtight seal.

Plastic film *See* Cling film

Plastic sheeting
Heavy-weight plastic sheeting can be used as a wrapping material. It should be sealed with masking tape or freezer tape.

High-density plastic sheeting is not suitable for wrapping food but is ideal for interleaving between food items, making them easy to separate after freezing.

Sealing *See* Freezer tape, Heat sealing, Twist ties

Smells
Smoked fish and curries, as well as foods containing garlic, onions, strong herbs or spices, should be overwrapped so that odours and flavours don't permeate ice, ice cream or other foods.

Storage areas
It is worthwhile to set aside certain areas of the freezer for particular types of food.

This will enable you to find food easily and to keep the freezer tidy.

Tins

Rust-free tins are good containers for storing fragile items such as decorated cakes.

Line with plastic and seal lids with tape for long-term storage.

Twist ties

Twist ties are paper- or plastic-covered wires that close plastic bags tightly. They are sold in bundles or by the metre in supermarkets, department stores and gardening stores. They are also supplied with packets of oven bags.

Twist ties with metal content should be removed before putting the food in the microwave oven.

String or an elastic band could be used instead.

Vacuum pumps

A vacuum pump is an essential piece of equipment; it removes air from filled plastic bags easily and effectively.

Air remaining in bags after sealing causes frost to form on the food and may result in freezer burn.

Pumps are available from electrical goods shops, hardware shops and kitchenware departments of department stores.

No vacuum pump? To expel those last gasps of air in a plastic bag, plunge the bag into icy water before you twist-tie the tops.

Waxed paper

Waxed paper is not recommended for outer packaging. It is not moisture- or vapour-proof, and deterioration of the food will result if it is used. However, it can be used to interleave foods such as pancakes or steaks which need to be separated easily and which are then packaged with other material.

DEFROSTING
AND
REHEATING

Frozen food must be correctly and carefully defrosted so that its quality can be maintained; however, it is certainly not a complex process and there are only a few things you need to know.

Many foods can be defrosted either in the refrigerator or at room temperature. Using the refrigerator is slower but safer, especially for large pieces of food, because the food is less likely to be affected by bacteria. If food is to sit at room temperature, it must be a cool room temperature. Any food that needs longer than 3 hours to defrost at room temperature could be potentially unsafe and should ideally be defrosted in the refrigerator.

These days it is increasingly common to use a microwave oven to defrost and reheat food, and indeed if you own both a freezer and microwave it is only sensible to make them work together for maximum efficiency. Using a microwave oven means that frozen food can now be defrosted in minutes instead of hours.

For more detailed information than this chapter provides, see also *Microwave Hints*, the companion volume in this series.

Some foods are best cooked from frozen or can be cooked from frozen as an option. Vegetables are the best example; small fish are another.

Baby food

Baby food must be thoroughly defrosted, then heated to a high temperature, allowed to cool and used immediately.

Do not reuse any leftovers.

Meat in cooked dishes has a freezer life of 1-2 months; fruit and vegetables, 3-6 months.

Defrost in the refrigerator for 3-4 hours, then reheat thoroughly and allow to cool before serving. Use immediately.

Bread

A small loaf of bread takes about 1 hour to defrost at room temperature, a large loaf 2 hours and rolls 20 minutes.

Frozen bread can be toasted without being defrosted.

Rolls can be reheated from frozen in a hot oven.

Cakes

Cakes, bread and bread products, buns, scones, biscuits and pastry items should be placed on absorbent kitchen paper to absorb moisture during microwave defrosting.

Cooking from frozen

Most foods can be cooked from frozen, and prepared items such as fish fingers, beefburgers, raw pastry and vegetables are best cooked this way.

Whole chickens must be thoroughly defrosted before cooking. If the oven heat doesn't penetrate right to the bone, germs might possibly cause food poisoning.

A whole frozen chicken won't cook from frozen without burning on the outside before the meat near the bone has fully defrosted.

Meat can equally be cooked from frozen or defrosted first. Defrosted meat will take less time to cook, but cooking from frozen is the best way to keep meat juicy.

Frozen joints being cooked from frozen must be tested with a meat thermometer to ensure that they are properly cooked.

Test the meat about 20 minutes before the end of cooking time.

Beef should have reached 77°C (well done) or 66°C

(rare); lamb, 82°C (well done) or 77°C (pinkish); and pork, 88°C (well done).

Checking the temperature will enable you to calculate how much more cooking time is needed.

Chops or steaks being grilled or fried can easily be cooked from frozen but should be cooked more slowly than usual.

Cooking from frozen times

To calculate cooking times from frozen for beef, allow about 55 minutes per 500 g at 180°C for well-done and 50 minutes for rare beef.

For lamb, allow about 60 minutes per 500 g at 180°C.

For pork, allow about 60 minutes per 500 g at 200°C.

Dairy food

Milk should be defrosted in the refrigerator.

Yoghurt should be defrosted for about 1 hour at room temperature.

Cheese should be defrosted for 24 hours in the refrigerator and allowed to stand until it reaches room temperature before serving.

Butter or margarine should be defrosted at room temperature. Allow about 4 hours per 250 g.

Separated eggs should be defrosted in the refrigerator.

Defrost cream in the refrigerator, allowing 24 hours, or at room temperature.

Defrosting food

Cover food closely while it is defrosting.

Do not defrost food in a warm environment as this provides ideal conditions for bacteria to multiply. Choose a cool place, such as a kitchen cupboard, or defrost in the refrigerator.

Always throw away the liquid from defrosting meat and poultry; it must never be allowed to contaminate other food.

Do not refreeze food once it has defrosted unless it has been subsequently cooked. Raw meat can be

successfully cooked and refrozen.

Never refreeze any food that has been defrosted accidentally over a period of days.

See individual entries for specific types of food in relevant chapters for more detailed information.

Defrosting in the microwave oven

Food can be defrosted in the microwave in a fraction of the time it would take to defrost conventionally, but it is essential that it defrosts gently and evenly.

When food is defrosted, the small ice crystals melt first and if defrosting in the microwave is too rapid, parts of the food will start to cook before the areas of large ice crystals have defrosted. It is best to defrost food on the LOW or DEFROST setting.

If your microwave does not have a LOW or DEFROST setting you can defrost manually by turning off the oven every 30 seconds and allowing the food to stand for 1½ minutes before turning it on again for another 30 seconds.

The number of micro-waving and resting times will depend on the size and amount of food being defrosted — the larger the item, the longer the periods of heating and resting.

Dense foods like joints of meat need a standing time of at least 15-20 minutes at the end of defrosting.

Turn foods over during defrosting and separate small items as soon as possible.

Break up liquid or semi-liquid foods with a fork and shake or fork apart vegetables and small fruit.

Stand foods such as breads, cakes and pastries on absorbent kitchen paper to absorb the moisture.

Emergencies

Unexpected guests at dinner time? No microwave to speed up defrosting? Here are some (slightly bizarre) emergency ideas:

Put the package of food to be defrosted in your dishwasher and set it on the DRY setting.

Put the package on a rack within the oven so that air can circulate around it more easily — but don't turn the oven on!

The low setting of your blow-dryer directed at under and around the package might do the trick.

Sprinkle a generous amount of salt on the package, then put the package in salted water.

Obviously none of these emergency ideas will be of any use with a leg of lamb, but smaller parcels of, say, sliced raw chicken will defrost relatively quickly.

Fish

Whole fish are best defrosted in unopened wrappings at room temperature before cooking.

Small fish and fillets or steaks are best cooked from frozen.

Fruit

If fruit is to be served without further preparation, defrost it slowly in its container, unopened, to prevent it becoming too soft and mushy.

Fruit that tends to discolour should be defrosted rapidly and kept submerged in its syrup during defrosting.

Allow 6-8 hours per 500 g for defrosting in the

refrigerator or 2-4 hours at room temperature.

Frozen fruits usually have a lot of juice after thawing; to avoid soggy pies or damp cake fillings add a little thickening such as cornflour or arrowroot, or drain off excess juice.

Large items

If large items of food begin to defrost unevenly small pieces of foil may be used to cover any areas which appear to be developing hot spots or beginning to cook during microwave defrosting.

Metal ties

Remove metal twist ties from bags and replace with string or an elastic band before putting the bags in the microwave.

Meat

Meat can be cooked from the frozen state and frequently this is preferable as meat which is allowed to defrost will lose a great deal of its moisture content as well as losing food value and flavour. This applies particularly to the smaller cuts of meat that are to be grilled or pan-fried.

However, meat that needs further preparation before cooking will need to be defrosted, as will large joints which may prove difficult to cook from frozen.

When defrosting is necessary it is best carried

out in the refrigerator with the meat still in its packaging material. Allow 6-8 hours per 500 g for a large joint. Small pieces of meat will defrost more quickly. When defrosting by microwave oven follow the oven manufacturer's instructions.

When small cuts of meat are cooked directly from the freezer allow a little longer cooking time. Cook the meat initially at a high temperature, sealing the surfaces, then reduce the heat and continue cooking until done.

Meat that has been defrosted in the refrigerator can be stored for several days, unpackaged, in the meat keeper.

Rolled joints such as breast of lamb must be defrosted before cooking, because all surfaces of the meat would have been handled and rolled up, so thorough cooking is necessary in order to destroy bacteria which might be present.

Chops, steaks and sausages can be easily cooked from frozen and so can diced meat for casseroles and kebabs. Start the cooking at a lower than usual temperature and cook for almost twice as long, increasing the temperature halfway through.

For best results, pot-roast and boiling joints should be defrosted before cooking.

Mincemeat can be cooked from frozen. Allow extra cooking time.

Casseroles and pre-cooked pies can be reheated from frozen but they should have been frozen in shallow pie dishes, so that there is less risk that they will not heat right through when reheated.

Offal must always be completely thawed.

Meat and poultry

Meat will defrost faster if you place it, still wrapped and sealed, in a sink full of lukewarm water. The cold of the parcel will quickly chill the water (which you might need to change after a few minutes). Don't be

tempted to use really hot water — the defrosting would be too rapid and uneven.

Microwave defrosting

Always underestimate defrosting times. Many foods will still be icy in the centre when removed from the microwave, but will melt through during the standing time. If necessary, food can be returned to the microwave for further defrosting.

Only defrost food in the microwave if it is going to be cooked and eaten immediately.

For faster and more even defrosting, separate frozen foods, such as chops and fish cutlets, into pieces as they defrost.

Turn food over if possible during defrosting. If this is not possible, rearrange individual items or turn the dish around.

Shake or gently break down fruit during the defrosting and standing time.

Microwave defrosting times

Times can vary according to the density and frozen temperature of the food and the power of your microwave oven.

When increasing or decreasing quantities alter the defrosting times accordingly.

Check the food regularly — twice as much food does not necessarily mean twice the defrosting time.

Packaging

Open cartons and slit plastic pouches before microwave defrosting or reheating.

Flex pouches and packagings which cannot be broken up or stirred to distribute the heat during microwave defrosting.

Pastry

Pastry can be reheated or freshly baked from frozen.

Place it in a hot oven direct from the freezer and cook for about 15 minutes longer than an unfrozen pie.

Cooked pies to be eaten cold can be defrosted at room temperature in 1½-2 hours.

Poultry

Whole chickens weighing more than 2 kg should be defrosted in the refrigerator for 1-1½ days. Chickens weighing less than 2 kg will need 12-16 hours.

Ducks weighing 1.5-2.5 kg will need 1-1½ days to defrost in the refrigerator.

Geese weighing 2-7 kg will require 1-2 days to defrost in the refrigerator.

Turkeys weighing more than 8 kg will take 2-3 days and less than 8 kg 1-2 days in the refrigerator.

Poultry — microwave defrosting

Pour off the liquid from frozen poultry which is being microwave defrosted in its original wrapping.

This liquid absorbs microwave energy and slows down the defrosting process.

Finish defrosting poultry in cold water in its original closed plastic bag, rather than trying to defrost it completely with microwave energy, otherwise it may start to cook around the outside before it is fully defrosted in the centre.

Remember to remove giblets from defrosted poultry before serving.

Running water

You can speed the process of defrosting by holding food under cold running water.

The food should be packed in rigid plastic containers with well-fitting lids.

When you have loosened the food in the container, you can then remove it and reheat slowly in a saucepan.

Skins

Pierce the skins of such foods as sausages before defrosting in a microwave oven.

Vegetables

Vegetables are best cooked directly from the freezer without being defrosted, except corn on the cob, which benefits from partial defrosting in the refrigerator.

SOUPS, SAUCES AND CEREALS

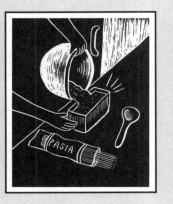

Soups and sauces often take time and trouble to prepare. However, if you cook in bulk and freeze them, you will always have them handy when you want them. Basic sauces are especially useful because they can form the foundation of so many different sauces. The defrosting and reheating of soups and sauces are absolutely straightforward.

When making soups and sauces for freezing, do not over-season when cooking. More can always be added when defrosting and reheating. Milk, cream or eggs should always be added to soup after freezing, not before. Garlic is another ingredient best added after freezing; its flavour tends to deteriorate after a couple of weeks in the freezer.

Both fresh pasta and cooked pasta dishes freeze and reheat very well. Pasta dishes are especially convenient to have in the freezer because they can be reheated in the oven without being defrosted first.

Apple sauce

Place 500 g peeled, cored and sliced apples in a saucepan with 2-3 tablespoons water and cook gently, uncovered, until soft and thick (about 10 minutes). Beat the apples to a pulp, then purée in a blender. Stir in 1 tablespoon butter and a little sugar if the apples are tart.

To freeze, pour into rigid containers in portions of about 250 g.

Béchamel sauce

If béchamel sauce is made with milk it will separate when defrosted. Try this recipe, which uses stock.

Melt 30 g butter in a heavy saucepan, blend in 30 g flour and cook, without allowing to brown, over a gentle heat for 5 minutes. Add 500 ml stock gradually, stirring well until the mixture is smooth. When all the liquid has been absorbed, bring to the boil briefly and season. Allow to cool, and when cold pour into rigid containers in useful portions (say, 250 ml) and freeze.

Cheese sauce

Cheese sauce should be frozen in convenient quantities of about 250 or 500 ml. After cooking cool quickly, stirring occasionally to prevent a skin forming. Freeze in rigid containers, leaving a 1 cm headspace.

Cheese sauce has a freezer life of 3 months. Reheat gently from frozen. Do not allow to boil and stir to prevent separation.

Cooling

Soups and sauces must be cooled rapidly before freezing. First stand the pan in cold running water and then, when all traces of steam have gone, pour the liquid into the freezing container and chill in the refrigerator before freezing.

Freezer life

Soups and sauces may be stored for 2-3 months, but if highly seasoned they should be used within 2-3 weeks. Recipes containing chopped bacon should be used within 6 weeks.

Mint sauce

To freeze, pour into rigid containers, allowing headspace, or ice cube trays. When hard transfer cubes to plastic bags.

Mint sauce has a freezer life of 6 months. Defrost at room temperature for about 30 minutes; thin with a little water if necessary.

Pasta

Fresh pasta of all types can be frozen easily and keeps well. However, there is little point in freezing it since it cooks so quickly. Freezing cooked pasta dishes is more useful.

Cook pasta in the usual way but keep it slightly undercooked. Drain, cool in running water, shake dry and pack in plastic bags, then freeze.

Cooked pasta has a freezer life of 1 month and composite dishes 2-3 months.

See also Reheating pasta

Pesto genovese

Make sure the container is firmly sealed before freezing because pesto has a penetrating smell.

Pulses

Some pulses, such as lentils, dried beans and peas, take a long time to soak and cook, so it can be useful to cook a lot and freeze them for future use.

Soak and cook pulses in the usual way but remove from heat when still slightly undercooked and allow to cool completely. Drain, pat dry and pack into rigid containers.

Pulses have a freezer life of 6 months.

Defrost at room temperature for 3-4 hours, then add to other dishes (e.g. soups or casseroles), giving the pulses enough time to cook properly.

Reheating pasta

Add frozen pasta to a saucepan of boiling water. When the water returns to the boil, drain and serve.

To reheat pasta dishes, remove the lid or covering

and reheat in the oven without defrosting at 180°C for about 1 hour or until heated through. If drying out seems to be a risk, the top could be loosely covered with foil.

Reheating sauces

White sauce can be reheated slowly in a thick pan or double boiler and beaten with a wooden spoon.

Apple sauce can be defrosted at room temperature.

Other sauces should be reheated gently in a double boiler or non-stick pan. Adjust the seasoning if necessary.

Reheating soups

Pour hot water over the outside of the rigid container to loosen the contents.

Some soups tend to separate on reheating; avoid this by heating slowly at first, stirring frequently or beating with a wire whisk.

Reheating is the time to add milk, cream, eggs or garlic to frozen soups.

Reheating stock

Stock should be reheated gently from frozen and diluted as required.

Rice

Rice freezes very well but since it takes so long to defrost and reheat, and so little time to cook fresh, there is no point in freezing it.

Risotto

When the risotto is cooked cool it and pack in rigid containers.

Risotto has a freezer life of 2 months.

Defrost it overnight in the refrigerator, then reheat it gently in the top of a double-boiler.

Roux

To make and freeze roux for sauces, see chapter 10, 'Dairy products and eggs'.

Sauces

Sauces should be frozen in convenient quantities of about 250 ml in rigid containers, leaving about 1-2 cm headspace.

White and brown sauces have a freezer life of 6 months; tomato sauce, 1 year; meat, curry and bread sauce, 3 months; apple sauce, 1 year.

White sauce can be reheated slowly in a thick pan or double boiler and beaten with a wooden spoon. Apple sauce can be defrosted at room temperature.

Other sauces should be reheated gently in a double boiler or non-stick pan. Adjust the seasoning if necessary.

See also Cooling, Freezer life, Reheating

Soups

Soups with a milk base do not freeze satisfactorily.

Vegetable, chicken, lentil and other dried legume soups are excellent when frozen. Other soups that freeze really well include onion, split pea and all the various chowders.

Clear broths (chicken, turkey or beef) freeze satisfactorily. Do not add noodles or rice when planning to freeze these soups; add them when reheating.

Barley, pasta and potato generally freeze badly within soups. Add these ingredients at the reheating stage, precooked if necessary.

Soup thickened with ordinary flour will curdle on reheating, so use cornflour (which gives a creamy result) as a thickening agent.

Soups may be stored in rigid containers, freezer-safe glass jars or plastic bags. It is sensible to divide the soup into convenient portions of about 250 ml before freezing.

For an unusual croûton, toast one side of several slices of French bread, then spread a mixture of grated cheese, melted butter, egg yolk and herbs on the other side and toast. After the croûtons are cooked and cool, either cut into smaller pieces or leave as whole pieces, then pack in bags, seal and freeze. Thaw at room temperature and toss into an onion or vegetable soup.

See also Cooling, Freezer life, Reheating

Stock
Strain and cool the cooked stock and remove excess fat. To economise on freezer space boil the stock down as far as possible and freeze concentrated stock in ice cube trays.

Pack the cubes in plastic bags and return to the freezer.

Stock has a freezer life of 6 months.

See also Reheating stock

White sauce *see* Béchamel sauce

MEAT

Meat needs little preparation before freezing except for trimming off any excess fat. If possible, remove bones from the meat as they take up space in the freezer. It might be best to ask the butcher to cut up large joints into smaller pieces, such as chops, for separate, easy packing. It is important to choose high-quality raw meat for storage, either fresh or frozen, as freezing does not improve cheap meat in flavour or texture.

When freezing meat ensure that it is packaged correctly, because if any air comes into contact with frozen meat, it can cause freezer burn. Pad any bones with foil so that they don't puncture the wrappings. Chops and steaks should be open-frozen or interleaved with waxed paper before wrapping in plastic for easy separation.

Meat should be frozen rapidly or it will coarsen, and the subsequent loss of juices during defrosting will result in a loss of flavour. Set your freezer controls to fast-freeze 24 hours beforehand and don't freeze more than a tenth of your freezer capacity in any 24 hours.

Meat that has been thawed should never be refrozen raw. Cook it, and then refreeze it safely.

Bacon

Only freeze bacon that is perfectly fresh. Pack rashers in 250 g quantities closely wrapped in foil or cling film, then overwrapped in plastic bags.

The faster bacon is frozen right through the better it will be, so freeze it in small lots (no more than 2 kg) only.

Rashers wrapped in foil and plastic have a freezer life of 8 weeks if smoked, 3 weeks if unsmoked; wrapped joints, 8 weeks smoked, 5 weeks unsmoked. Vacuum packs, smoked and unsmoked, have a freezer life of 25 weeks. Defrost overnight in the refrigerator.

All frozen bacon should be cooked as soon as it has thawed.

Beef

Wipe the meat with a damp cloth and trim off excess fat (fat turns rancid in the freezer).

Steaks should either be wrapped individually in plastic or interleaved with waxed paper and then wrapped in plastic. Mince should be packed in plastic in small quantities (500 g or 1 kg). Cut stewing meat into pieces and pack tightly in plastic bags.

Meat that is to be marinated or simmered and chops or steaks can be used straight from the freezer.

If defrosting meat, leave the meat in its wrappings and allow at least 5-6 hours in the refrigerator or 2½-3 hours at room temperature per 500 g.

If defrosting steaks, allow 1-2 hours at room temperature. If roasting a joint from frozen, cook it slowly and allow an extra 14-18 minutes per 500 g.

Beef — cooked

Casseroles, stews, shepherd's pie, meatballs, meat sauces and steak and kidney pies can all be frozen.

Cook until just tender and remove any surplus fat from the surface when cool.

Finish cooking from frozen at 180°C for 45 minutes.

Casseroles

Casseroles to be frozen should only be cooked for about three-quarters of the usual time before freezing — reheating will complete the cooking.

There must be plenty of sauce so that the meat is covered and will not dry out.

Root vegetables, other than onions, should be added towards the end of the cooking time as they become mushy.

Garlic should be added when reheating as its flavour deteriorates rapidly in the freezer.

When the casserole is part-cooked and cooled, remove

surplus fat from the top before freezing.

To freeze a large quantity, several times your usual meal size, place the cooked casserole in a roasting tin. Open-freeze until almost solid, then mark the servings with a knife. When completely solid cut into brick-like pieces with a freezer knife, wrap each one in foil, label and stack in the freezer. Reheat slowly from frozen when required.

Left-over wine can be frozen and later added to a casserole while still frozen. Pour it into ice cube trays or rigid containers, leaving headspace. Wine has a freezer life of 2 months.

Casseroles have a freezer life of 6 weeks if bacon, ham or pork are used and 4 months for other meats.

Reheat casseroles slowly from frozen.

Chicken liver

Cut off any greenish marks from the bile sac, wash, dry and pack in small quantities in cartons or plastic bags. Defrost in the refrigerator.

Chicken liver has a freezer life of 3 months if raw and 2 months if cooked.

Chops

Chops — lamb, pork or veal — can be cooked successfully from frozen. They should be interleaved with waxed or freezer paper or open-frozen and packed in small quantities in plastic bags.

Pork chops have a freezer life of 3 months; lamb, 6 months; veal, 6 months.

Chops must be cooked more gently than usual if cooked from frozen.

To defrost, leave them in their wrappings in the refrigerator overnight.

See also Lamb, Pork, Veal

Cooked meat

Cooked chopped meat (ham, chicken, turkey or beef) can be frozen tightly wrapped in plastic bags. Slice cooked meat to be eaten cold can be frozen if slices are interleaved with waxed paper and frozen in

rigid containers. Sliced meats in gravy or a complete meal with meat, gravy and vegetables can be frozen in a covered foil container. There must be plenty of gravy so that the meat is covered and will not dry out.

Cooked meat has a freezer life of 2 months.

Meat to be eaten cold can be defrosted in its container in the refrigerator.

Meat with gravy and vegetables should be heated from frozen in a 200°C oven for about 40 minutes. Loosen the cover before heating.

Ham

Ham has a limited freezer life because its high salt

content will make it turn rancid quickly. It won't turn bad, but it won't taste very pleasant.

Cooked ham can be cut in thick slices separated by greaseproof paper, then packed tightly in a plastic bag.

Chopped ham can be packed in plastic bags or rigid containers.

Uncooked ham is best stored whole, closely wrapped in foil and overwrapped in a plastic bag.

Cooked ham has a freezer life of 1 month; uncooked ham, 2 months.

Sliced or chopped ham should be defrosted in its wrappings in the refrigerator for about 3 hours; whole ham for about 5 hours per 500 kg.

Kidneys

Remove the fat and thin skin from fresh kidneys, then wash and dry them before freezing.

Spread on a tray and open-freeze, then pack into a plastic bag or interleave with waxed paper, overwrap in plastic bags and freeze.

Ready-frozen kidneys must be put in the freezer immediately after purchase.

Kidneys have a freezer life of 3 months.

They can be fried gently from frozen or defrosted before use.

Lamb

A lamb carcass comprises a variety of cuts for roasting, grilling and stewing, and there can be considerable saving in bulk-buying.

Most butchers will pack and label the meat ready for the freezer.

If you package it yourself, wrap the meat closely and extract as much air as possible before sealing.

Lamb has a freezer life of 6 months.

It can be cooked from frozen or defrosted slowly in the refrigerator, allowing about 5 hours per 500 g.

To roast frozen lamb allow 60 minutes per 500 g at 180°C.

See also Casseroles, Chops

Liver

Liver freezes well whether raw or cooked. Wash thoroughly, remove any blood and tubes, dry and slice. Interleave the slices with waxed paper, pack into plastic bags and freeze.

If freezing cooked liver, pack the slices in a foil container and make sure they are covered with sauce and gravy. Cover and freeze.

Liver has a freezer life of 3 months if raw and 2 months if cooked.

Defrost slices of raw liver in the refrigerator. Separate and cook as soon as they begin to soften. Cooked liver can be reheated from frozen covered with foil.

See also Chicken liver

Meat loaves
Cooked meat loaves can be frozen in a double layer of foil or freezer bags. They should be thawed out slowly in the refrigerator.

When making meat loaves to be served hot, only cook for two thirds of the stated cooking time. They will complete the cooking time when being reheated.

Meat pies
Cooked meat pies can be frozen, but before filling you should brush the bottom crust with melted butter to prevent sogginess. Wrap in foil or in a plastic bag to freeze.

Another method is to cook the meat filling, then put it in a foil container and cover with fresh pastry.

To freeze, wrap in foil or a plastic bag.

Mince
Pack the mince into plastic bags, choosing a bag one size larger than seems necessary, extract the air and seal.

Press the mince out flat, so that it fills the plastic bag in a thin layer.

See also Beef

Oxtail

Oxtail can be frozen raw or cooked. Chop the tail into joints (or get the butcher to do it), trim off surplus fat, pack into plastic bags, seal and freeze.

Alternatively, braise the oxtail and make it into soups. When cold, skim off surface fat, pack into rigid containers, leaving 1-2 cm headspace, seal and freeze.

Oxtail has a freezer life of 3 months if raw and 2 months if cooked.

Paté

Paté has a short freezer life because most meat or liver patés contain bacon.

Make the paté, cool, cover the top with foil and freeze.

The paté could also be turned out of the dish, wrapped in foil and frozen, or sliced and each slice wrapped individually.

The slices should also be overwrapped before freezing.

Paté containing bacon has a freezer life of 1 month; others, 3 months.

Defrost paté overnight in the refrigerator or for 6 hours at room temperature.

Pork

Trim off surplus fat, pad any bones and wrap the meat tightly in foil or plastic bags. Chops should be open-frozen or interleaved with waxed paper before wrapping in polythene for easy separation. Pack the meat as closely as possible to the freezer walls to ensure rapid freezing.

Pork has a recommended freezer life of 6 months.

It can be defrosted in the refrigerator in its wrappings, allowing 5 hours per 500 g, or cooked from frozen at 180°C, allowing 60 minutes per 500 g.

Frozen chops should be placed a little further from the heat than usual when being grilled.

Quail
Cut off the head and neck of quail and take out the crop. Pack in plastic bags

or, if more convenient, on foil trays, overwrapped in plastic bags. Seal and freeze.

Quail has a freezer life of 6 months.

Defrost quail in the refrigerator, allowing 5 hours per 500 g, before roasting.

Rabbit
Rabbit must be frozen when absolutely fresh. Cut it into large joints, pack in plastic bags and freeze.

Rabbit has a freezer life of 6 months.

Defrost rabbit in its wrapping in the refrigerator, allowing 5 hours per 500 g.

Sausages

Freshly made sausages and sausage meat may both be frozen.

Pack in plastic bags in convenient 250 or 500 g quantities, seal and freeze.

If you are making your own sausages, don't season them too highly and never add salt before freezing.

Sausages have a freezer life of 6 months.

Sausages can be defrosted in the refrigerator and grilled, or partly defrosted to separate them and then grilled, or cooked in a moderate oven. Sausage meat can be defrosted in the refrigerator before cooking.

Sliced meat

Many Thai and other Asian recipes require very thinly sliced meats, as does Italian carpaccio. When a recipe calls for thinly sliced meat, partially freeze the whole piece until it is very firm. With a sharp knife you will easily be able to cut thin slices.

Steak

Trim excess fat from steaks and then open-freeze. Wrap each steak flat in plastic or interleave with a piece of waxed paper and pack two or three together in a plastic bag. Seal and place in the coldest part of the freezer so that they will freeze rapidly.

Steaks have a freezer life of 6 months.

Defrost steaks in the refrigerator in their wrappings or cook from frozen. When grilling frozen steak, place it further away from the heat than usual.

Stews *see* Casseroles

Sweetbreads
Sweetbreads should be washed thoroughly, then left to soak in cold water for several hours. Pull off as much of the enclosing filament as possible,

remove the tubes, trim and rinse again and pat dry. Wrap each piece in plastic or freezer paper, then pack into plastic bags or rigid containers.

Sweetbreads have a freezer life of 3 months. Defrost in the refrigerator and use as required.

Veal
Veal freezes well. It has a freezer life of 6 months and can be defrosted overnight in the refrigerator.

FISH AND POULTRY

All fish and shellfish must be really fresh if it is to be frozen. It should preferably be frozen on the day it is caught.

All fish should be thoroughly washed, gutted and the scales removed. Larger whole fish freeze best if they are covered with ice — a method known as ice glazing. Smaller whole fish can be open-frozen. Some types of fish can be dipped in brine before freezing. Fish steaks and fillets should be interleaved with freezer wrap or cling film before wrapping in plastic bags.

Only young, fresh tender poultry should be frozen. If possible turn the freezer down to its lowest setting or turn on the fast-freeze switch at least 24 hours beforehand. Once the poultry is frozen return the temperature to its normal setting. Poultry should be wrapped carefully and securely because it is prone to freezer burn.

Never handle cooked or uncooked poultry together. Do not cut them up with the same utensils or use the same boards without thoroughly washing the boards and utensils.

Boiling fowls

Boiling fowls do not need defrosting before cooking.

Place the bird in a large pan with enough water to cover, season, then bring to the boil and simmer gently. When tender, cool the stock quickly, then package and freeze in suitable quantities for soup and sauces.

The layer of fat that accumulates at the top can easily be removed from the frozen stock before use.

Brine-dipping *see* Dipping

Chicken

Only plump, young tender birds are worth freezing raw. Others are better cooked before being frozen.

Purchased ready-frozen chickens should be put in the freezer quickly after buying.

To freeze a fresh whole chicken, truss and tie the legs to the body. Don't use skewers as they will tear the wrapping. Pack in plastic bags or wrap in foil.

Giblets should be packed separately if they are to be frozen.

Do not stuff chickens before freezing as the stuffing inhibits thorough defrosting.

Chicken pieces should be wiped with a damp cloth and wrapped individually in waxed or freezer paper. Overwrap all pieces in a plastic bag and freeze.

Chicken has a freezer life of 1 year.

Chicken must be defrosted properly in the refrigerator before cooking. Allow 24 hours in wrappings.

Chicken pieces will defrost (in their wrappings) in 4-6 hours in the refrigerator.

See also Chicken pieces, Cooked chicken, Giblets, Stuffing

Chicken pieces
Chicken pieces may be cooked straight from the freezer, but allow extra time to ensure thorough cooking.

Pack chicken pieces for freezing in a single layer in plastic bags. Remove air and package as for whole birds.

Before freezing a whole uncooked chicken breast that you'll probably use in a stir-fry anyway, slice it into stir-fry-size pieces.

It will freeze faster and can be cooked later in a semi-frozen state.

The same applies to casseroles; pre-cut the chicken into casserole-size chunks before freezing.

Uncooked chicken pieces have a freezer life of 4 months.

Crumbed chicken pieces should be placed on a tray and open-frozen for an hour or two, then packed into plastic bags. They have a freezer life of 4 months.

Cooked chicken pieces can be frozen in plastic bags or containers, then reheated on an oven tray when required. They have a freezer life of 2 months.

Cooked chicken

When cooking chicken dishes destined for the freezer, cool them as rapidly as possible when cooking is complete by standing the dish in iced water and stirring the contents from time to time, or by cooling slightly, then refrigerating until cold enough to package and freeze.

Cooked chicken dishes have a freezer life of 3 months.

Leftover meat from a roasted or boiled chicken should be cooled quickly, then taken from the bones and stored in a plastic bag or container, to be used in a variety of cooked dishes, sandwiches and salads.

Crab

Shellfish is highly perishable and must be

caught, cooked and frozen on the same day.

Cool the cooked crabs, remove all the edible meat from the shell and either pack the brown and white meat in separate containers or arrange the meat for serving in cleaned crab shells.

Cover with moisture-proof paper, overwrap in plastic bags and freeze.

Crab has a freezer life of 1 month.

Defrost for 6-8 hours in the refrigerator.

Crayfish

Drop crayfish into boiling salted water (1 tablespoon salt per litre of water).

Cook gently for 10-20 minutes, depending on size.

Drain well by hanging the tail over the sink or a bucket.

Open and clean the crayfish. Remove all edible flesh and package in watertight containers.

To prevent crayfish from drying, cover with a light brine solution (1 table-spoon salt per litre of water) and freeze quickly.

To freeze crayfish in its shell, package it in a plastic bag, then wrap in several thicknesses of clean news-paper. Place the parcel in another plastic bag, seal and label. This extra packaging will prevent sharp claws piercing the plastic.

Crayfish has a freezer life of 1 month and should be defrosted in the refrigerator for 6-8 hours.

Dipping fish

Steaks and fillets of lean fish can be prepared for freezing by dipping them in a cold salt solution (dissolve ½ cup salt in 1 litre water). Then drain, wrap and seal the fish.

Brine-dipped fish has a freezer life of 2 months.

Do not dip oily fish in brine.

Oily fish will last longer in the freezer if dipped for 1 minute in a solution of ¨ teaspoon crushed ascorbic acid dissolved in 1 litre cold water. Then drain, wrap and seal.

Duck

Young ducks with pliable breastbones and flexible beaks are best for freezing.

Older birds can be frozen but would be better cooked first.

Wipe inside and outside with a damp cloth and chill in the refrigerator before freezing.

Truss the duck but don't use skewers as they will tear the packaging.

Pack in a plastic bag, expelling as much air as possible, and freeze.

Giblets should be washed, dried and packed separately for freezing.

Duck has a freezer life of 6 months; giblets, 2 months.

Defrost duck in its wrappings in the refrigerator for 24 hours.

Fish

Fish must be caught and frozen ideally on the same day but certainly within 24 hours, so it is not advisable to freeze fish bought in shops.

Small fish should be scaled, gutted and gills and fins removed. Heads and tails can be left on.

Wash thoroughly in cold running water and drain. Wrap closely in a plastic bag, seal and freeze.

Large fish are best cut into fillets or steaks and made up into shallow packages. They freeze faster this way and will be more useful when you want to cook them.

Remove the head, tail and fins, clean the belly cavity, wash thoroughly in cold running water and drain.

Either divide into fillets or cut it across the bone into 2 cm steaks. Wrap closely in a plastic bag and freeze.

If you want to serve a large fish whole, wrap it in heavy-gauge plastic or foil, or ice-glaze it.

Thawing fish immersed in milk is a good idea as this process removes any of the 'frozen' aftertaste.

Dishes made with cooked fish can be frozen and reheated successfully.

Fish frozen at home has a freezer life of 3 months for white fish; oily fish, 2 months; cooked fish dishes, 1 month.

Small fish, fillets and steaks can be cooked from frozen. A whole large fish can be defrosted for 24 hours in a cool place.

Cooked fish dishes can be reheated from frozen.

See also Dipping; Fish fillets; *individual entries for fish and shellfish*; *and* Ice glazing *and* Open freezing *in* chapter 1, 'Freezer basics'

Fish fillets

One fillet can be cut from each side of a fish. The skin can be removed from fillets if desired. Egg and crumb coating can be applied before freezing.

If you are going to apply batter or egg and crumb coating to frozen fish fillets before cooking they must be defrosted first, as coatings will not stick to a frozen surface.

Defrost the fillets in
their packaging in the
refrigerator.

Giblets
Chicken and goose giblets
should be frozen separately
from the rest of the bird.

They have a freezer life
of 2 months.

Geese
Geese are normally sold
ready to cook or frozen.
However, if you are freezing a fresh one, choose a
goose with not too much fat.

Cover the bones with foil
and pack the whole bird in
a plastic bag, extracting as
much air as possible before
sealing. Pack the giblets
separately.

Because it contains so much
fat goose does not have a
long storage life. It should
only be frozen for up to 4
months.

Defrost at room
temperature for about
18-24 hours.

See also Giblets

Haddock *see* Smoked fish

Ice glazing *see* chapter 1, 'Freezer basics'

Kippers *see* Smoked fish

Mussels
Mussels should be cooked
before freezing. Like all

shellfish, they must be very fresh when frozen.

Make sure they are tightly shut; any remaining open or with broken shells should be discarded.

Wash well in several changes of water, scrubbing the shells with a stiff brush, remove any fibrous matter and place the mussels in a large saucepan.

Cover with a damp cloth and place over a moderate meat until they open — about 3 minutes.

Allow to cool, then pack with or without shells in plastic bags or rigid containers with their own juice.

Mussels have a freezer life of 1 month.

Defrost in their wrappings overnight in the refrigerator and use as required.

Oily fish *see* Dipping

Open-freezing *see* chapter 1, 'Freezer basics'

Oysters
Oysters should be frozen the same day they are taken from the water.

Wash the outside of the shells and open carefully, retaining the juice.

Wash in salted water, drain and pack in rigid containers with the strained juices. Leave 1-2 cm headspace for expansion, cover and seal.

Oysters have a freezer life of 1 month.

Defrost raw oysters in the refrigerator in their unopened container for 6-8 hours.

Cooked oysters can be added to hot soup or sauce straight from the freezer.

Prawns

Prawns must be absolutely fresh when frozen.

Wash thoroughly, boil in lightly salted water until they turn pink (2-4 minutes) and cool in the liquid. Shell, pack tightly in plastic bags, seal and freeze.

Prawns can also be frozen raw. Remove the heads, wash in salted water, drain and pack into plastic bags, seal and freeze.

Prawns have a freezer life of 1 month.

Cooked prawns can be defrosted in the refrigerator if required for salads or added to cooked dishes while still frozen.

Raw prawns can be dropped into boiling, lightly salted water and simmered for 2-4 minutes after the water has returned to the boil.

Salmon

Salmon must be absolutely fresh when frozen and preferably frozen on the same day it is caught.

Scale the fish, wash thoroughly under cold running water, drain and dry.

Leave it whole or cut it into two or three joints, or remove the head and tail and cut it across the bone into 2 cm steaks.

Wrap in heavy-duty plastic and freeze.

If you want to freeze the fish whole it should be no more than 5 cm thick, and it should preferably be ice-glazed, then returned to the freezer wrapped in heavy-duty plastic.

Salmon has a freezer life of 2 months.

Defrost a whole fish and large joints slowly in their wrappings in a cool place.

A whole salmon will take up to 24 hours.

Salmon steaks can be cooked from frozen to defrost.

See also Smoked fish

Scallops

Scallops should be frozen on the same day as they are taken from the water.

Scrub the outside of the shells thoroughly. Place them in a hot oven for a few minutes and remove as soon as the shells open. Take off the black outer fringe around the scallop. Wash the fish in salted water. Cut it away from the shell with its orange roe, rinse and drain.

Pack into rigid containers, cover and freeze.

Scallops can also be frozen as a cooked dish.

Scallops have a freezer life of 1 month.

Defrost in the fridge overnight and use as fresh scallops or place in hot water or sauce from frozen to defrost and cook.

A cooked dish can be reheated from frozen.

Shellfish
Shellfish must be absolutely fresh when frozen and have a freezer life of 1 month.

The shells of crayfish and prawns can become very offensive if they have to be left in the dustbin for several days before collection. Instead, after shelling, wrap in several thicknesses of newspaper and tie or tape the parcel, then freeze until garbage collection day.

Smoked fish
Smoked fish such as salmon, kippers or haddock can be wrapped and frozen,

and will keep in the freezer for 2 months.

Stuffings

Any recipe for stuffing may be frozen. Divide into required amounts and pack in plastic bags, seal and freeze.

If stuffing is to be baked separately, pack in foil dishes, seal and freeze.

Dry forcemeat stuffing mix can be packed in plastic bags and frozen. When needed the amount required may be removed and mixed with fat and eggs.

Completed stuffing has a freezer life of 1 month; dry mix, 6 months; stuffings containing sausage meat, 2 months.

Completed stuffings can be defrosted in the refrigerator overnight then added to poultry or fish and cooked.

Dry stuffing can be used from frozen.

Trout

Trout must be absolutely fresh for freezing.

Gut the fish and remove the head, tail and fins if necessary. Wash well under cold running water and drain.

Wrap each fish closely in a plastic bag, expelling as much air as possible, seal and freeze.

Trout has a freezer life of 2 months and can be cooked from frozen.

Turkey

A ready-frozen turkey should be put in the freezer as soon as possible after buying.

Leftover roast turkey can be sliced and frozen. Interleave the slices with moisture-proof paper and pack them tightly together in a rigid container or plastic bag to prevent drying out.

Alternatively, the meat can be chopped, mixed with a sauce and frozen in rigid containers for later use in cooked dishes.

Use the carcass to make stock or soup, both of which can be packed in rigid containers and frozen. *See also* Soups, Stock.

Turkey has a freezer life of 6 months if uncooked and 1 month if cooked.

An uncooked turkey should be defrosted completely in the refrigerator before cooking.

Defrosting time takes 2-4 days, depending on the size of the bird.

Cooked meat to be eaten cold should be defrosted in its container in the refrigerator; meat in sauce can be reheated from frozen.

Whiting

Whiting must be absolutely fresh before freezing.

Scale the fish, rinse thoroughly, then gut. The head and tail can be left on.

Wash thoroughly in cold running water and drain.

Wrap each fish closely in a plastic bag to exclude as much air as possible and freeze.

Whiting has a recommended freezer life of 3 months and can be cooked from frozen or defrosted in the refrigerator.

VEGETABLES

Most vegetables freeze successfully except for those with a very high water content, such as lettuce and cucumber. All vegetables to be frozen should be young and tender, and they are best picked and frozen in small amounts. Vegetables are best blanched before freezing, which involves dipping them briefly in either boiling water or steam to destroy the enzymes within them that make the food deteriorate. Blanching also helps to preserve colour, flavour, texture and nutritional value.

Some vegetables, particularly those belonging to the marrow family, retain their texture and flavour better if they are cooked before freezing, rather than by blanching. Potatoes are also preferable in a cooked rather than a blanched state.

Pack vegetables only in quantities suitable for your needs or for special recipes. Vegetables should not be refrozen or reheated.

Alfalfa

Alfalfa tends to lose its crispness in the freezer but it is still perfectly acceptable for use in cooked dishes.

To freeze fresh alfalfa, pack it straight into plastic bags, expelling as much air as possible before sealing. It has a freezer life of 2 months. To defrost, leave in the refrigerator for 3-4 hours before using.

Artichokes (globe)

Remove the outer leaves, wash thoroughly and trim the stems. Blanch in boiling water for 7 minutes, then plunge immediately into ice-cold water. Drain and cool completely, then pack into plastic bags.

Globe artichokes have a freezer life of 1 year. Allow to defrost overnight in the refrigerator or for 4-5 hours at room temperature. Alternatively, cook from frozen in water with a little lemon juice (to prevent discoloration) for 10-15 minutes until tender.

Artichokes (jerusalem)

Jerusalem artichokes are best frozen as a purée.

Scrub and peel, cut into small pieces and cook gently with butter and stock until tender. Purée in a blender and pack into rigid containers, leaving a 2 cm headspace.

Jerusalem artichoke purée has a freezer life of 3

months. It can be reheated from frozen.

Asparagus

Wash, trim and sort the spears into sizes. Blanch small spears for 2 minutes, medium spears for 3 minutes and large spears for 4 minutes. Drain and cool, then pack in rigid containers, leaving a 2 cm headspace.

Asparagus spears have a freezer life of 9 months.

Asparagus need not be thawed before cooking. Cook it in boiling water for 2-4 minutes.

Aubergine *see* Eggplant

Beansprouts

Beansprouts do not freeze successfully because they lose their crispness and become soggy, but they can be used in cooked dishes.

Blanch for 1 minute, then drain and cool. Dry as much as possible, then pack into rigid containers or plastic bags.

Beansprouts have a freezer life of 2 months.

Defrost in the refrigerator for 3-4 hours before using.

Beetroot

Beetroot can be frozen whole or sliced.

Wash well, then cook in boiling water until tender for 5-10 minutes (small beets) and 45-50 minutes (larger beets). Drain and allow to cool, then rub the skins off. Pack small beats into plastic bags and slice large ones into rigid containers.

Beetroot has a freezer life of 6 months.

Leave to defrost in unopened containers in the refrigerator for 6-8 hours or at room temperature for 2-4 hours.

Broad beans

Blanch podded broad beans for 3 minutes, then cool and drain. Pack in rigid containers or plastic bags. Alternatively, open-freeze on trays then tip into plastic bags and seal.

Broad beans have a freezer life of 12 months.

They can be cooked from frozen in boiling water.

Broccoli

Blanch trimmed broccoli spears for 3 minutes, then plunge into cold water, drain and pack into plastic bags or rigid containers.

Broccoli has a freezer life of 1 year and can be cooked from frozen in boiling water.

Brussels sprouts

Trim off any discoloured or wilted leaves, then wash and blanch the sprouts for 3 minutes. Plunge them into ice-cold water. Drain and place on flat trays and open freeze. When frozen, tip the sprouts into plastic bags and seal.

Brussels sprouts have a freezer life of 1 year and can be cooked from frozen in boiling water for 4-8 minutes until tender.

Cabbage

Wash the cabbage thoroughly and blanch it in boiling water for 1-2 minutes. Plunge it into ice-cold water, drain and pack in plastic bags. It can be diced or shredded before freezing if desired.

Cabbage has a freezer life of 6 months.

It can be cooked from frozen for 5-8 minutes.

Capsicum *see* Peppers

Carrots

Although carrots are available all year round, young baby carrots could be frozen for later use. They can be frozen whole or sliced. If freezing whole, remove tops, wash and scrape them, then blanch for 3 minutes. Sliced carrots should be blanched for only 2 minutes. Cool in ice-cold water, drain and pack into plastic bags, expelling as much air as possible before sealing.

Carrots have a freezer life of 1 year and can be cooked from frozen in boiling water or in a little butter and stock.

Cauliflower

Cauliflower can be frozen either blanched or cooked.

Remove leaves, wash and divide into florets about 5 cm in size. Blanch in boiling water with the juice of 1 lemon for 3 minutes. Plunge into cold water, drain and allow to cool. Place the florets in plastic bags, seal and leave a 2 cm headspace and freeze.

Alternatively, open-freeze on trays before storing in plastic bags.

Cauliflower has a freezer life of 6-8 months. Cook it from frozen in boiling water and simmer for 4 minutes until tender.

Cauliflower cheese

Cook the cauliflower until tender, then cover with cheese sauce. Place in a rigid container and leave to cool completely, then seal, leaving a 2 cm headspace and freeze.

Cauliflower cheese has a freezer life of 6 months.

Defrost in a refrigerator for 2-3 hours, then cook in a moderate oven until heated through and golden brown.

Celery

Celery is only suitable for cooking after freezing because it loses its crunchy texture.

Wash thoroughly and trim the stalks, removing any tough fibres, then cut into small lengths — about 5 cm long — and blanch for 2 minutes. Allow it to cool, then drain and pack into plastic bags.

Celery has a freezer life of 1 year.

It can be cooked from frozen.

Chives
Snip small quantities of fresh chives into plastic bags, containers or ice cube trays and freeze.

Frozen chives have a freezer life of 6 months.

Use them straight from the freezer because they retain their former texture and quickly soften.

Chokos
Chokos can be either boiled or baked before freezing.

Method 1: Cook until tender in boiling water. Drain well, then mash and pack into plastic containers with well-fitting lids, leaving 2 cm headspace. Cool, then freeze.

Method 2: Peel and remove seeds, then bake in a moderate oven until barely tender. Allow to cool, then pack in plastic bags or containers.

Choko has a freezer life of 6 months.

Boiled choko should be defrosted, then reheated over boiling water. Drain any excess liquid that accumulates before serving.

Baked choko should be placed on an oven tray directly from the freezer and returned to the oven until tender.

Courgettes *see*
Zucchini

Cucumber
Raw cucumbers do not freeze satisfactorily because they contain a high proportion of water and become very mushy when thawed. However, they can be frozen either puréed or cooked.

Method 1: Peel a raw cucumber, chop and blend until smooth, then pour into rigid containers and freeze.

Method 2: Place baked cucumber in rigid containers and freeze.

Cucumber has a freezer life of 2 months.

Defrost at room temperature for 1-2 hours.

Eggplant
Eggplant can be frozen when cut into slices and blanched. Peel and slice, then blanch for 4 minutes, drain and cool. Pack in layers in rigid containers leaving a 2 cm headspace.

Alternatively, pack in plastic bags, expelling as much air as possible before sealing.

Eggplant has a freezer life of 1 year.

French beans
Young, thin French beans freeze best but larger ones may also be frozen if they are not stringy.

Wash, trim both ends and blanch for 1-2 minutes. Cool, drain and open-freeze on trays.

When firm, pack into plastic bags, expelling as much air as possible before sealing.

French beans have a freezer life of 1 year and can be cooked from frozen.

Garlic

Garlic cloves can be frozen, but chopped or crushed garlic should not be frozen because it tends to develop an unpleasant flavour.

Avoid using garlic in cooked dishes which are intended to be frozen as the flavour tends to deteriorate and affect the taste of the finished dish. Garlic should be added when the dish is reheated.

Wrap garlic cloves in foil or freezer wrap, then overwrap in a plastic bag.

Garlic cloves have a freezer life of 3 months and can be defrosted in a few minutes at room temperature.

Ginger

Root ginger deteriorates quite quickly in the open air. Peel a fresh piece, freeze it and grate off ginger as required.

Herbs

Most fresh herbs freeze successfully.

Wash and dry herbs before freezing. When dry pack the sprigs into plastic bags.

Alternatively, chop finely and freeze in small plastic containers or bags.

Herbs can also be frozen in ice cube trays covered with a little water, then transferred to plastic bags.

Frozen chives and parsley can be grated as required and then put back into the freezer.

You can freeze sprigs of mint to put into fruit cup drinks. Mint loses quality when frozen, but is perfectly adequate when used in this way.

Herbs have a freezer life of 6 months and can be added to most dishes straight from the freezer.

Juices

Prepare vegetable juices in the usual way, then pack into plastic containers leaving about 2 cm headspace.

Some juices may separate when defrosted but can easily be stirred or blended together again.

Vegetable juices have a freezer life of 6 months.

Kohlrabi

Young, tender kohlrabi may be blanched and frozen.

Trim the bases, leaves and stalks and wash well. Blanch whole in boiling water for 3 minutes, cool and drain. Open-freeze on trays until firm, then transfer into plastic bags and freeze.

Kohlrabi has a freezer life of 1 year.

It can be cooked from frozen in boiling water.

Kumaras *see* Sweet potatoes

Leeks
Leeks may be frozen but will only be suitable for use in cooking, such as soups and casseroles.

Trim the ends and outer leaves, then wash thoroughly. Blanch whole in boiling water for 3-4 minutes, then cool, drain and pack into plastic bags.

Thicker leeks can be sliced into chunks and blanched

for 2 minutes, before packing into plastic bags.

Leeks have a freezer life of 6 months.

They can be cooked from frozen in boiling water for 7-10 minutes or added to soups or casseroles.

Lentils *see* chapter 4, 'Soups, sauces and cereals'

Lettuce
Lettuce does not freeze well because of its very high water content. However, it can be used in soups that can be frozen successfully.

Mixed vegetables
Mixed vegetables can be prepared, blanched for 1 minute and frozen, then packed together in plastic bags.

Choose vegetables that are similar in size, or chop larger pieces into neat dice.

Mixed vegetables have a freezer life of 6 months.

Cook directly from the freezer in boiling water.

Mushrooms

Freeze button mushrooms whole and larger ones sliced for use in cooked dishes. Wipe with a damp cloth until clean.

Spread whole button mushrooms on trays and open-freeze until firm. Transfer into plastic bags and seal, expelling as much air as possible, and return to the freezer.

Slice larger mushrooms and sauté in a little butter for 1 minute.

Pack into small rigid containers with their cooking liquid, allow to cool completely and freeze.

Raw mushrooms have a freezer life of 1 month and cooked mushrooms 3 months.

They can be used from frozen if added to stews, soups or sauces, or if sautéed and used as a vegetable.

Alternatively, defrost in the refrigerator in their containers for about 6 hours.

Nuts *see* chapter 8, 'Fruit'

Olives

Transfer olives to small cartons and cover with cold water, adding a few drops of lemon juice. Leave a 2 cm headspace and seal securely.

Olives have a freezer life of 6 months.

Defrost at room temperature for 3-4 hours, then consume within 3 days.

Onions

Peel, chop or slice large onions and pack into rigid containers.

Overwrap carefully with plastic wrap or a plastic bag, so that they do not taint other foods in the freezer with their smell.

Peel and blanch small onions for 3 minutes. Cool, drain and pack into plastic bags. Overwrap with another bag in order to prevent cross-flavouring.

Chopped onions have a freezer life of 3 months and whole baby onions 6 months.

Chopped onions should defrost in their wrappings for 15 minutes at room temperature before using. Use whole onions from frozen.

Parsnips

Parsnips should be washed, trimmed, peeled and cut into narrow strips.

Blanch in boiling water for 2 minutes, cool, drain and

open-freeze on trays until firm. When firm, transfer the parsnips into plastic bags to store.

Parsnips have a freezer life of 1 year.

If parsnips are to be boiled they may be cooked from frozen. If they are to be roasted, allow to defrost at room temperature for 3-4 hours before cooking.

Peas

Remove the shells from fresh peas, then blanch in boiling water for 1-2 minutes. Cool quickly in ice-cold water, drain and open freeze on trays until firm. Pack into plastic bags, expelling as much air as possible.

Fresh and commercially frozen peas have a freezer life of 1 year.

Cook from frozen in boiling water.

Snow peas should be blanched in boiling water for 2-3 minutes, cooled, drained and open-frozen on trays until firm. Pack into plastic bags.

Peppers

Red, green and yellow peppers may be frozen.

Wash thoroughly, cut off the stems and remove all the seeds and inner membranes.

Cut into halves, slices or rings and blanch in boiling water for 2 minutes (slices or rings) or 3 minutes (halves). Cool in ice-cold water and drain. Pack into plastic bags, expelling as much air as possible.

Peppers have a freezer life of 1 year.

Either defrost in their wrappings for 1-2 hours at room temperature or use directly from the freezer in cooked dishes (e.g. casseroles).

Potatoes

Most potatoes can be frozen successfully either fully or partially cooked.

Potato croquettes should be open-frozen on trays until solid, then transferred to rigid containers. Separate the layers with greaseproof paper.

Partially fry homemade chips until just soft (about 2 minutes), cool, open-freeze, then pack into plastic bags, expelling as much air as possible.

New potatoes should be small and all of similar sizes. Cook until just undercooked, drain, cool and pack into plastic bags.

Roast potatoes should be cooked as usual, drained on absorbent paper, cooled and packed into polythene bags.

Frozen chips have a freezer life of 6 months and all other types of potatoes 3 months.

Potato crisps left over after parties will stay fresh and

crisp if frozen in sealed containers.

Defrost croquettes at room temperature for about 1 hour, then deep-fry or bake. Deep-fry chips from frozen. Cook roast potatoes from frozen in a fairly hot oven; fry them quickly in a little oil to make them crisp again. Small new potatoes can be cooked from frozen but larger ones should be defrosted.

Pulses *see* chapter 4, 'Soups, sauces and cereals'

Pumpkin
Wash the pumpkin, peel, cut in half and remove all the seeds.

Cut into small pieces and either steam or boil until tender. Either drain and allow to cool, or mash with butter until thoroughly puréed and allow to cool. Pack in rigid containers and leave a 2 cm headspace.

Pumpkin has a freezer life of 1 year.

Pumpkin pieces will defrost in 3-4 hours in the refrigerator.

Pumpkin purée may be reheated gently from frozen before using.

Purées
Cook one or several varieties of vegetable in boiling salted water until tender. Drain, mash or sieve, then pack into plastic containers leaving about 2 cm headspace. Small

quantities can be frozen in ice cube trays and packed in plastic bags after freezing.

A large amount of puréed pumpkin, a popular first food for babies, is ideal for freezing in ice cube trays.

Put all the cubes of frozen food into a container and withdraw one or two to thaw and then feed to a small-appetite infant as needed.

Vegetable purées have a freezer life of 6 months.

Reheat in a double saucepan.

Red cabbage *see* Cabbage

Runner beans

Cut off the ends of runner beans and remove strings if necessary. Slice thickly because they lose their taste and texture if sliced too finely. Blanch in boiling water for 2 minutes, cool in cold water, drain and open-freeze on trays in the freezer. When firm, transfer to plastic bags and withdraw as much air as possible before sealing.

Runner beans have a freezer life of 1 year and are best cooked from frozen in boiling water.

Salad vegetables

Salad vegetables, including cucumbers, lettuce, tomatoes, radishes and spring onions, do not freeze well because they contain a high proportion of water and become soft and mushy when thawed.

Snow peas *see* Peas

Spinach
Spinach freezes well but it is more convenient to cook it before freezing.

Strip the leaves from the stalks and place in a large saucepan. Add 1-2 tablespoons water and cook for 1-2 minutes until the leaves start to wilt, or pour boiling water over the spinach and stand for 1 minute, then drain. Squeeze out the moisture until the spinach is as dry as possible, then allow it to cool.

Chop finely and pack into plastic bags, expelling as

much air as possible before sealing.

Spinach has a freezer life of 1 year.

It should be reheated gently from frozen until defrosted and heated through.

Spring onions
Spring onions do not freeze well because of their high water content.

Squash
Peel the squash, remove any seeds and cut into chunks. Blanch in boiling water for 1-2 minutes, plunge into cold water, drain and cool. Pack into plastic bags and expel as much air as possible before sealing.

Alternatively, squash may be fully cooked and puréed before freezing in rigid containers, leaving a little headspace.

Squash has a freezer life of 1 year.

Blanched squash may be cooked from frozen in boiling water. Purée should be allowed to thaw at room temperature for 3-4 hours before using.

Swedes *see* Turnips

Sweetcorn

Sweetcorn can be frozen whole, as corn on the cob or in kernels.

Remove any leaves or silk threads. Trim off the stems and blanch whole cobs in boiling water for 4 minutes (small), 6 minutes (medium) and 8 minutes (large). Plunge into cold water, drain, cool and pat dry with kitchen paper. Pack whole cobs into plastic bags, extracting as much air as possible before sealing.

Alternatively, blanch as before and allow to cool. Strip off all the kernels with a knife and open-freeze on trays in the freezer. When firm transfer into plastic bags and extract as much air as possible.

Sweetcorn has a freezer life of 1 year.

Whole cobs may be cooked from frozen in boiling water, or defrosted at room temperature for about 1 hour.

Cook kernels from frozen in boiling water for about 5 minutes.

Sweet potatoes

Sweet potatoes may be frozen after being parboiled, completely cooked or made into a purée.

Wash, peel and cut into slices or chunks. Slices should be parboiled and allowed to cool, then packed tightly into rigid containers.

Sweet potatoes have a freezer life of 6 months.

Partly and fully cooked sweet potatoes may be heated from frozen.

Allow purée to thaw at room temperature for 2-3 hours before gently reheating.

Tomatoes

Tomatoes collapse completely when thawed so they cannot be eaten raw after freezing. However, they can be used in cooking.

Method 1: Freeze whole tomatoes by placing them in boiling water for a few seconds, then peeling away the skin. Allow them to cool, then pack in rigid containers or tightly in plastic bags.

Method 2: Cut in half, open-freeze until firm then transfer to plastic bags.

Alternatively, freeze tomatoes as purée. Cover with boiling water to loosen the skins, then peel and remove the pips and hard core. Simmer gently without any extra water for 5 minutes until soft. Blend until smooth. Cook and pack into small containers.

Whole tomatoes have a freezer life of 10-12 months and purée 6-8 months.

Whole tomatoes may be used from frozen in soups and casseroles. Defrost tomato purée in its container for 2-3 hours at room temperature before using.

Tomato juice *see* Juice

Turnips

Trim and peel the turnips. Leave small ones whole but dice large ones. Blanch whole turnips in boiling water for 4 minutes, diced turnip for 2 minutes. Allow to cool, drain and pack into plastic bags, extracting as much air as possible before sealing.

Turnips may also be frozen as a purée. Trim, peel, dice and cook until tender. Drain, mash and allow to cool. Pack into rigid containers, leaving a 2 cm headspace before sealing.

Whole turnips have a freezer life of 9-12 months and purée 8-10 months.

Blanched turnips can be cooked from frozen in

boiling water. Cooked turnips may be reheated gently from frozen.

Vegetables in sauce

To freeze vegetables in sauce, slightly undercook the vegetables then cool and fold into the sauce. Pack into rigid containers. Vegetables in sauce have a freezer life of 2 months.

Zucchini

Use smaller zucchini; larger ones do not freeze well because they contain too much water.

Wash, trim both ends off and cut into thick slices. Blanch for 1 minute, cool, drain and open freeze on trays until firm, then pack in plastic bags.

Alternatively, zucchini can be sautéed in butter instead of blanched and packed into rigid containers when cool, leaving a 2 cm headspace.

Zucchini have a freezer life of 1 year.

Blanched zucchini can be cooked from frozen.

FRUIT

Fruit tends to change in consistency in the freezer more than any other food. Generally, the juicier the fruit, the more it will soften on defrosting. The best results are obtained from fully flavoured fruits, particularly berries; blander fruits such as pears have little flavour. However, most fruit can be frozen somehow.

Fruit can be frozen as a purée or in a syrup pack, a dry sugar pack or a dry pack (see chapter 1, 'Freezer basics'). Most fruit that tends to discolour is best frozen in a syrup, as is fruit that contains little juice. Juicy fruit is best stored in a dry sugar pack, and overripe fruit is best frozen as purée. Other types of fruit, such as grapes, gooseberries and rhubarb, are most successfully frozen in a dry pack in rigid containers.

Some fruit can be frozen in its raw state, but that which discolours readily, such as peaches, nectarines and apples, should be treated with an anti-oxidant like ascorbic acid or lemon juice before freezing. Blanching will prevent discoloration, and fruit that is completely cooked before freezing will not discolour.

Apples

To freeze apples, wash, peel and core.

Method 1: Cut up into small pieces and stew, sweetened or unsweetened, with a minimum of water until soft. Then sieve or liquidise and allow to cool. Pack the purée into rigid containers or plastic bags.

Method 2: Slice the fruit into a bowl of salted water, then rinse and pack with sugar in alternate layers into rigid containers. Allow 500 g sugar for every 1.5 kg fruit, and leave 1 cm headspace.

Baked apples may also be frozen. Cook them as usual, then allow to cool completely and freeze unwrapped until firm.

Pack the apples into a rigid container and divide them with a sheet of greaseproof paper.

Apple slices have a freezer life of 12 months; apple purée, 6 months and baked apples, 3 months.

To defrost, leave apple slices or purée in an unopened container at room temperature. If they are to be heated no defrosting is necessary. Heat baked apples through from frozen at 190°C for 20 minutes.

Apple juice *see* Fruit juice

Apricots

Apricots are best frozen either whole (with the stone

removed) or sliced in a syrup. An unstoned fruit may develop an almond flavour around the stone if kept frozen for a long time.

Alternatively, freeze apricots as a purée.

Wash and dry the fruit, plunge into boiling water for 30 seconds and then peel.

Method 1: Remove the stones and slice into a syrup made with 500 g sugar to 1 litre water with 1-2 tablespoons lemon juice (to prevent discoloration). Place the fruit in a rigid container and immerse in the syrup by placing crumpled foil over the top before seasoning.

Method 2: Keep the fruit whole and immerse in cold syrup as in method 1.

Method 3: Purée cooked fruit, either sweetened or unsweetened, then pack into rigid containers.

Apricots in syrup have a freezer life of 9-12 months; apricot purée has a freezer life of 6-8 months.

To defrost, leave in an unopened container either in the refrigerator for 6-8 hours per 250 g or at room temperature for 2-4 hours.

Avocado
Avocados tend to lose their flavour and texture if frozen whole, but they can be frozen pulped for use in dips and sauces.

Peel and mash, adding 1 tablespoon lemon juice to each avocado, then pack in small containers.

Avocado has a freezer life of up to 2 months. To defrost, leave to stand at room temperature in the unopened container for about 2 hours; use immediately.

Bananas

Bananas turn black when frozen unless treated with lemon juice.

Method 1: Peel and mash ripe bananas with ½ cup lemon juice to each kilo of fruit. Pack into plastic containers leaving about 2 cm headspace.

Method 2: Peel bananas and chop into large pieces.

Roll the pieces in lemon juice. Pack into plastic bags, expel the air, seal, label and freeze. Use in banana puddings.

Method 3: Peel firm bananas, dip in lemon juice, then into egg and breadcrumbs. Freeze in a single layer in a plastic container. Use for frying for chicken Maryland or similar dishes.

Method 4: Peel and wrap ripe bananas individually in cling film. Serve to children as ice blocks straight from the freezer.

Frozen bananas are also relieving for teething babies to suck and chew on.

Mashed bananas have a freezer life of 6 months;

chopped bananas, 2 months; whole bananas in egg and breadcrumbs, 2 weeks; bananas in cling film, 2-3 days.

Blackberries

Choose dark, black berries for freezing and avoid those with large, woody pips.

Method 1: Pack whole fruit with 125-175 g sugar per 500 g fruit, mix well and pack into rigid containers, leaving a 2 cm headspace.

Method 2: Pack berries into rigid containers without sugar.

Method 3: Pack the berries into rigid containers with syrup made with equal quantities of sugar and water.

Blackberries may also be puréed with 125 g sugar per 500 g fruit and used as a sauce for desserts.

Blackberries have a freezer life of 8-12 months in sugar or a syrup pack; purée has a freezer life of 6-8 months.

To defrost, stand overnight in the refrigerator.

Candied peel

Candied citrus peel can be frozen either in large pieces or chopped up.

Pack the peel tightly into plastic bags or foil, excluding as much air as possible.

Frozen candied peel has a freezer life of up to 1 year. Defrost at room temperature for 3-4 hours.

Cherries

Cherries freeze well, but the stones should be removed before freezing because the cherries may develop an almond flavour around the stone.

Remove the stalks, then wash and dry the cherries.

Method 1: Open-freeze on trays until firm, then transfer the fruit to plastic bags.

Method 2: Pack in dry sugar, allowing 250 g sugar to every 1 kg fruit.

Method 3: Place in rigid containers with a sugar syrup made with 500 g sugar to every litre of water.

Frozen cherries have a freezer life of 9-12 months (dry sugar or syrup pack) or 1 year (open-freeze).

Allow to defrost very gently in an unopened container at room temperature for about 3 hours.

Use immediately, otherwise the fruit becomes discoloured.

Cherries in a syrup can be reheated gently from frozen.

Chinese goose-berries *see* Kiwi fruit

Coconut

Grate or shred coconut, moisten it with coconut milk and then pack it into plastic bags.

Thaw for 2 hours at room temperature, drain off the milk and use for fruit salads, icings or curries.

Coconut has a freezer life of 2 months.

Cumquat *see* Kumquat

Dates
Both fresh and dried dates may be frozen. Remove the stones from fresh dates, pack into plastic bags and freeze.

Remove dried dates from their original packaging and freeze in plastic bags.

Both fresh and dried dates have a freezer life of 1 year.

Allow to defrost at room temperature for about 2 hours.

Dried fruit
Most dried fruit, including sultanas, figs and dates, can be frozen. Freezing keeps them plump and moist.

Wrap the dried fruit tightly in plastic bags or small packages of foil, sealing them securely.

Dried fruit has a freezer life of 1 year.

Defrost at room temperature on a flat surface for about 2-3 hours. Separate the fruit as it defrosts.

Feijoas
Slice the fruit and cover with a light syrup to which you have added 1/4 teaspoon ascorbic acid per litre of syrup. Pack into plastic

containers, leaving 2 cm headspace.

Feijoas have a freezer life of 6 months.

Figs

Wash and remove the stems with a sharp knife.

Method 1: Cover whole figs with a light syrup. Pack into plastic containers, leaving headspace.

Method 2: Stew with or without sugar as desired. Pack into plastic containers, leaving headspace.

Method 3: Cut into pieces and freeze without sugar. Pack into plastic bags, expel the air and freeze. Use for jam-making.

Figs have a freezer life of 6 months.

Allow to defrost at room temperature for about 2 hours.

Fruit juice

Most fresh fruit juices can be frozen in rigid containers quite successfully, but do not freeze in plastic or glass containers.

Purée the fruit until it is as liquid as possible. Strain finely and allow to drip into a bowl.

Sweeten to taste if desired and pack into rigid containers, allowing a 2 cm headspace.

Commercially prepared cartons of fresh fruit juice

can be frozen in their containers, but it is preferable to transfer them to rigid containers because they tend to expand and could therefore burst their original cartons.

Fruit juices may also be frozen in ice cube trays then packed in plastic bags.

Homemade fruit juice generally has a freezer life of 4-6 months. Commercial juices should be frozen according to the manufacturer's instructions.

Allow to defrost at room temperature for about 2 hours.

Ice block makers filled with real fruit juice then frozen make a very healthy alternative to commercial ice blocks, at a fraction of the price too.

Fruit purée

Fresh fruit purée can be frozen very successfully.

Stew fruit with a little water, strain and then sieve to make a purée.

Sweeten if desired. Pack the purée into rigid containers, leaving a 2 cm headspace before sealing and freeze until firm.

Fruit purée has a freezer life of 1 year.

Allow to defrost for several hours at room temperature in its container. Stir as it defrosts to break up the ice crystals.

Fruit salad

Any fruit suitable for freezing incorporated in a fruit salad may be frozen in a sugar syrup.

Dissolve 250 g sugar in 500 ml water, bring to the boil and leave to cool. If fruits that are likely to discolour are to be frozen, add the juice of 1 lemon or $\frac{1}{4}$ teaspoon ascorbic acid to the syrup. Add the chopped fruit to the syrup and pack into rigid containers. Leave a 2 cm headspace and place a piece of crumpled foil on top of the fruit to make sure that it is completely immersed in the syrup. Seal securely and freeze.

Frozen fruit salad has a freezer life of 1 year and should be defrosted overnight in the refrigerator.

Gooseberries

Wash the fruit, top and tail them, dry and freeze, packed into plastic bags.

Gooseberries have a freezer life of 6 months.

Grapefruit

Peel the grapefruit, remove all the pith and divide into segments.

Method 1: Dry pack by layering the fruit with 125-175 g sugar to every 500 g fruit and place in rigid containers.

Method 2: Syrup pack the fruit in a heavy syrup of 500 g sugar to every 500 ml water and pack in rigid containers leaving a 2 cm headspace.

Grapefruit has a freezer life of 1 year.

It can be defrosted overnight in the refrigerator.

Grapes

Grapes tend to become soft and mushy when defrosted.

Seedless grapes can be frozen whole, but other types should be skinned, halved and the pips removed.

Pack in a syrup, made with 250 g sugar to every 500 ml water, and place in a rigid container leaving a 2 cm headspace.

Grapes have a freezer life of 1 year and can be defrosted

at room temperature in about 2 hours.

Guavas

Wash the trim the fruit. Pack into plastic bags ready for jam and jelly making.

Alternatively, stew with sugar to taste and pack into plastic containers, leaving a little headspace.

Guavas have a freezer life of 6 months.

Allow to defrost at room temperature for about 2 hours.

Harvesting fruit

The ideal time to freeze most fruits is at the height of maturity. It is best to allow most fruits to reach this stage on the vine, bush or tree. However, fruits like peaches, plums and figs are apt to become soft on the plant and are easily bruised in handling. Gather such fruits in the 'firm ripe' stage and store overnight. This will ensure more even ripening and, like peaches, they will be easier to peel.

Gather fruit in the cool of the morning. Sun-heated fruit may bruise excessively from handling and result in an inferior frozen product.

Gather no more fruit than can be quickly prepared, packaged and frozen at one time. While speed of handling is not as critical with fruits as with vegetables, the shorter the holding time after gathering for most fruits, the better the frozen fruit will be.

Jam

Jam with a low sugar content (sometimes called freezer jam) may be frozen. Pack jam in small containers or plastic cartons. Do not use glass jars in the freezer because they are likely to shatter.

Jam has a freezer life of 3 months. Allow it to defrost in its container in a cool place overnight.

Kiwi fruit

Kiwi fruit may be frozen in syrup but becomes soft with the freezing and defrosting process and is only suitable for use in dishes.

Peel and slice the fruit into a syrup made with 250 g sugar to every 500 ml water.

Pack in rigid containers, leaving a 2 cm headspace.

Kiwi fruit has a freezer life of 1 year.

It can be defrosted at room temperature for about 2-3 hours.

Kumquat

Kumquat can be frozen either whole or chopped.

Either open-freeze on trays, then transfer to plastic bags, or pack in syrup in rigid containers, leaving a 2 cm headspace. Use a cold syrup of 250 g sugar to every 500 ml water.

Kumquat in a dry pack has a freezer life of 2 months or 1 year in a syrup pack.

Allow to defrost overnight in the refrigerator or for about 3 hours at room temperature.

Lemons

Wash and dry whole lemons and pack into plastic bags.

Alternatively, slice the lemons, spread on to trays and open-freeze. Then transfer to plastic bags, seal and return to the freezer.

Grated lemon rind may be packed into small cartons and frozen.

Lemons have a freezer life of 1 year.

Whole lemons should be unwrapped and defrosted at room temperature for 1-2 hours. Use slices frozen in drinks or defrost at room temperature for about 1 hour.

Grated lemon rind can be used frozen if allowed to defrost at room temperature for 30 minutes.

See also Oranges

Lemon juice
Lemon juice can be frozen in ice cube trays and used to flavour water drinks.

Lime *see* Lemons

Mandarins
Mandarins can be frozen for use in desserts.

Peel and remove the pith. Prepare a cold sugar syrup with 250 g sugar to every 500 ml water and pack the segments into rigid containers covered with the syrup. Leave a 2 cm headspace before sealing.

Mandarins have a freezer life of 1 year.

They can be defrosted overnight in the refrigerator or at room temperature for 3-4 hours.

Mangoes
Ripe mangoes can be frozen successfully in syrup.

Peel the fruit, remove the stones and slice. Pack in rigid containers covered with a cold syrup made with 500 g sugar to every litre of water. Place a piece of crumpled foil on top of the fruit to keep it immersed in the syrup, so that it does not discolour. Leave a 2 cm headspace and seal securely.

Mangoes have a freezer life of 1 year.

Defrost for 3-4 hours at room temperature or overnight in the refrigerator.

Marmalade

Marmalade keeps well and there is no need to freeze it.

If making marmalade from frozen oranges, remember that freezing lowers the pectin level of the fruit, so either add commercial liquid pectin or an additional one-eighth extra fruit.

When slicing limes, oranges, kumquats or lemons to make marmalade, freeze the fruits first for an hour or so. Then pare through the fruits with an ultra-sharp or an electric knife. No waste, no juice squirting everywhere.

See also Oranges

Melons

Firm, sweet melons freeze best. Watermelon is difficult to prepare for freezing because it has so many seeds.

Method 1: Cut the melon in half, remove the seeds and

cut the flesh into balls, cubes or slices, then wrap in plastic bags with a little sugar sprinkled over it.

Method 2: Make a syrup using 500 g sugar to every litre of water and pack into rigid containers, covering with the syrup. Place a piece of crumpled foil on top of the fruit to keep it immersed in the syrup and seal securely.

Frozen melon has a freezer life of 6 months.

Defrost in the refrigerator overnight or at room temperature for 2-3 hours.

Use when still slightly frosted.

Nectarines *see* Peaches

Nuts

Moist, fresh nuts can be frozen very successfully, as long as they're not salted. A bulk nut warehouse is the place to visit. Then package usable quantities and freeze them for up to a year. Toasted and buttered nuts only last around 3 to 4 months.

Nuts may be frozen in shells, whole, chopped, flaked or roasted.

Pack whole or chopped nuts in plastic bags or small rigid containers and seal well.

Whole and chopped nuts have a freezer life of 1 year and toasted nuts 4 months.

Defrost at room temperature for about 3-4

hours in containers or bags.

Nuts left over after parties will stay fresh and crisp if frozen in sealed containers.

Oranges

Oranges can be successfully frozen in a dry sugar pack or a syrup pack. Grate off the rind before freezing and pack it into small cartons or pieces of foil and freeze for future use as a flavouring or decoration. (*See also* Marmalade.)

If the oranges are to be used for marmalade freeze them whole in plastic bags. Otherwise remove the peel, pith and pips from the oranges and cut into slices or segments.

Method 1: Place alternate layers of fruit and sugar in rigid containers, using about 175 g sugar to every 4 oranges and freeze.

Method 2: Pack the prepared oranges in rigid containers in a sugar syrup made with 250 g sugar to every 500 ml water. Leave a 2 cm headspace before sealing.

Oranges have a freezer life of 1 year. Defrost in containers for about 3 hours at room temperature.

Orange and lemon peel is much easier to grate while still frozen.

Oranges and lemons can be frozen whole, unpeeled. When defrosted they are suitable for juicing.

Oranges cut into quarters and frozen can be served to children as ice blocks.

Papaya

Peel the fruit, remove the seeds and slice into a cold syrup made with 500 g sugar to every litre of water. Stir in 2 tablespoons lemon juice to each litre of syrup and pack in rigid containers.

Papaya has a freezer life of 9-12 months.

Defrost in containers at room temperature for about 1-2 hours.

Passionfruit

Scoop out the juice and flesh from the passionfruit. Make a cold syrup using 500 g sugar to every litre of water. Add 30 ml lemon juice and stir in the passionfruit. Pack into rigid containers and freeze upright until firm.

Passionfruit can also be frozen straight off the vine. They'll keep for about 12 months.

Passionfruit has a freezer life of 1 year.

Defrost the fruit in its container at room temperature for about 1-2 hours.

Pawpaw *see* Papaya

Peaches

Peaches are best frozen either in a cold sugar syrup or as a purée. Peaches discolour rapidly so it is best to put them directly into a sugar syrup.

Peel the peaches either under cold water or after a few seconds blanching if their skins are difficult to remove.

Method 1: Remove the stones, and slice the peaches into a syrup made with 250 g sugar to every 500 ml water. Add ¼ teaspoon ascorbic acid or 1 tablespoon lemon juice to help prevent discoloration. Pack into rigid containers and place a piece of crumpled foil on top of the fruit to keep it immersed in the syrup. Leave a 2 cm headspace before sealing with a lid.

Method 2: Purée the stoned peaches, add 1 tablespoon lemon juice and 125 g sugar to each 500 g fruit and pack into rigid containers.

Peaches in syrup have a freezer life of 9-12 months and puréed peaches 6-8 months.

Defrost peaches in their containers at room temperature for 3-4 hours, and then serve while still frosty.

Defrost purée at room temperature for 3 hours.

Pears
Pears are best frozen lightly cooked because raw pears tend to discolour quickly and lose their crisp texture and flavour.

Peel, quarter and core the pears. Dip into lemon juice immediately to prevent discoloration.

Prepare a syrup with 250 g sugar to 500 ml water and poach the pears in it for 1½ minutes.

Cool and pack the fruit into rigid containers.

Cover the syrup and place a piece of crumpled foil on the top to immerse the pears in the syrup.

Leave a 2 cm headspace before sealing with a lid.

Frozen pears have a freezer life of 1 year.

Defrost at room temperature for 2-3 hours.

Pineapples

Pineapples freeze very well either in a dry pack or in a syrup pack. Peel off all the hard skin, remove the hard core and slice or dice the fruit.

Method 1: Pack in sugar (about 125 g sugar to every 500 g fruit) in plastic bags, expelling as much air as possible.

Method 2: Pack pieces of pineapple in rigid containers and cover with a cold syrup made with 250 g sugar to each 500 ml water. Cover with crumpled foil in order the immerse the fruit in the liquid and leave a 2 cm headspace before sealing with a lid. Crushed pineapple can also be frozen in this way, using about 125 g sugar to every 375 g fruit.

Crushed pineapple has a freezer life of 8 months and pineapple in syrup up to one year.

Defrost in containers at room temperature for 3-4 hours.

Plums

Most varieties of plum freeze well. If stored for a long time the skins become tough and the stones taint the flesh, so it is best to remove the stones and stew the fruit gently or pack them in syrup.

Wash and halve the fruit and remove the stones.

Method 1: Pack into rigid containers and cover with sugar syrup made with 250 g sugar to every 500 ml water. Place a piece of crumpled foil on top of the fruit to keep it immersed in the syrup.

Method 2: Gently stew the fruit with sugar and allow it to cool completely, then pack into rigid containers leaving a 2 cm headspace.

Plums have a freezer life of 1 year.

Plums in syrup may be cooked from frozen.

Defrost stewed fruit in its container at room temperature for 2-4 hours.

Quinces

There is a considerable loss of flavour when frozen quinces are thawed.

The most satisfactory way to freeze them is to purée them well and flavour with sugar and lemon juice.

Raisins *see* Dried fruit

Raspberries
Raspberries freeze very well, keeping their colour and flavour. They may be frozen with or without sugar or as a purée.

Open-freeze whole raspberries on trays until firm, then transfer into plastic bags to store.

Alternatively, they may be packed with sugar, adding 125 g sugar to every 500 g fruit, and placed in plastic bags.

Make raspberry purée (adding sugar to taste) and pour it into rigid containers, leaving a 2 cm headspace before sealing.

Raspberries have a freezer life of 1 year.

Defrost whole fruit and purée at room temperature for about 3 hours.

Fruit that has been open-frozen may be used straight from the freezer.

Rhubarb
Do not freeze rhubarb with limp stalks.

Wash the rhubarb and remove the leaves and thick stalk bases.

Cut into 2 cm lengths and blanch in boiling water for

1 minute. Plunge into cold water, drain and cool.

Method 1: Open-freeze on trays and pack into plastic bags, expelling as much air as possible before sealing.

Method 2: Pack in rigid containers and cover with a sugar syrup made with 250 g sugar to every 500 ml water. Cover with a lid leaving a 2 cm headspace.

Rhubarb may also be stewed, sweetened and frozen as purée in rigid containers.

Rhubarb frozen in a dry pack has a freezer life of 6-8 months; as a syrup pack, 9-12 months and as a purée, 1 year.

Dry packed rhubarb can be defrosted at room temperature for a few hours or defrosted gently with a little water and sugar before cooking in desserts.

Defrost purée at room temperature for about 3 hours.

Strawberries

Whole strawberries lose their texture and their flavour alters if frozen.

Strawberry purée freezes extremely well and can be used, among other things, for making strawberry daiquiris.

Whole strawberries should be hulled, dusted clean but not washed, and placed on trays to open-freeze before packing in plastic bags or rigid containers.

Purée should be sieved into rigid containers with sugar to taste and sealed securely.

Strawberries have a freezer life of 1 year.

Whole fruit should defrost in its containers at room temperature for about 3 hours. It is best served when still frosty.

Defrost purée at room temperature for about 3 hours.

Sultanas *see* Dried fruit

Watermelon

Watermelon is difficult to prepare for the freezer because of the quantity of seeds.

It is better to make watermelon into fruit juice and freeze it that way. *See* Fruit juice.

DESSERTS AND BAKING

A great variety of desserts and baked foods can be frozen either before or after cooking: biscuits, bread, cakes, cake mixtures, croissants, crumpets, ice cream, pancakes, pancake batter, pies of all types, puddings, sorbet, waffles ...

As usual, there are some simple rules to be followed to obtain the best results, and care needs to be taken with preparation and packaging. Not all types of cake icing freeze equally well, for instance, and iced cakes need to be packed in rigid containers so that the icing is not spoiled in handling. Sponge cakes freeze well if you interleave the slices with waxed paper and if the filling is not added before freezing.

The convenience of freezing is particularly obvious in relation to cakes, breads and desserts. Delicious sorbets can be whipped up with great ease. A whole stack of pancakes can be frozen and the required number removed easily. A sliced loaf of bread can be frozen and a couple of slices peeled off when needed. Sponge cakes can be frozen, defrosted quickly and filled when guests arrive. When making homemade bread an extra loaf or two can easily be baked and frozen.

Batter

Pancake batter should be poured into rigid containers in either 250 or 500 ml quantities, leaving a 1-2 cm headspace.

Batter has a freezer life of 3 months and needs at least 2 hours to defrost.

See also Pancakes

Biscuits

All types of biscuits can be frozen unbaked or baked, and the quality after thawing remains high.

Pack the dough or baked biscuits in good-quality plastic bags or containers.

Frozen dough should be thawed at room temperature until soft enough to handle.

Most frozen biscuit dough may be sliced without thawing; some may need partial thawing in the refrigerator. Bake in the same way as fresh dough.

Biscuits have a freezer life of 3 months.

Bread (commercial)

If commercial bread is to be frozen for 1-2 weeks only, its original plastic wrapping may be used. For longer storage it should be over-wrapped with foil or plastic.

Overwrapped commercial bread has a freezer life of 3 months.

The crust of some bread separates from the body of the loaf on thawing. This tendency is more usual with breads that have a thick crust and cannot be avoided.

Bread (homemade)

Homemade bread and rolls should be prepared and baked as usual, then cooled quickly on a wire rack. Pack in plastic bags, seal and freeze.

Homemade bread has a freezer life of 3 months.

Frozen loaves may be thawed in their plastic wrappings at room temperature, or may be unwrapped and reheated in a slow oven for 20 minutes.

If the bread is wrapped in foil, it can be reheated in the foil wrapping.

Open the top of the packaging to allow the steam to escape for the last 10 minutes of reheating.

Rolls are best reheated in a slow oven for 15-20 minutes.

See also Sandwiches

Breadcrumbs
When you have stale bread or cake, turn it into crumbs and freeze it for use whenever crumbs are required.

If you have a blender, frozen sliced bread can be crumbed without being defrosted.

Cakes
Butter cakes may dry out slightly after 2 months in the freezer, and after 4 months flavour changes may be expected.

Angel cakes and sponge cakes freeze very well and will keep satisfactorily in the freezer for up to 6 months.

Coffee-, chocolate- and fruit-flavoured cakes freeze particularly well. Fruit cakes also freeze well; in fact their flavour continues to improve during freezing.

Synthetic essences like rum, coffee and vanilla develop an off taste in the freezer over time. Use real rum, real coffee or vanilla-bean flavoured sugar instead.

A cake will be ruined if it has been made with stale flour. While this will not be noticeable when the cake is fresh, stale flour deteriorates badly when the cake is in the freezer.

Sliced cake for packed lunches can be cut into portions and frozen with waxed paper between the portions. They can be placed in lunchboxes in the morning direct from the freezer and will defrost by lunchtime.

Small cakes can be packed in plastic bags in convenient quantities, but if they are iced they are better packed in boxes.

Either wrap sponge cake layers separately or put waxed paper between the layers before packing into a box or plastic bag.

Do not add jam or fruit fillings to sponge cakes before freezing as they will make the cake soggy.

Swiss rolls should be rolled up in cornflour rather than sugar if they are being frozen unfilled.

Cakes may be covered with buttercream icing before freezing but they will keep longer if they are not.

However, boiled icing, soft meringue icing and custard cream fillings do not freeze satisfactorily.

Cakes have a freezer life of 4 months for plain cakes and 3 months with buttercream icing.

Defrost sponge and layer cakes for 2 hours at room temperature and small cakes and buns for about 1 hour at room temperature.

Plain cakes can defrost in their wrappings, but iced cakes should be unwrapped to prevent the icing sticking to the surface and spoiling the icing.

See also Icing, Sponge cakes

Cake mixtures

Unbaked sponge and fruit cake mixtures can be frozen uncooked. Whisked sponge mixtures do not freeze well uncooked.

Line the tin in which the cake is to be baked with foil, place the mixture in it and freeze uncovered. When firm, remove from the tin, wrap the cake completely in foil, overwrap and return to the freezer.

When baking, remove wrappings but leave the foil lining.

Place the frozen cake in a preheated oven and bake for slightly longer than usual.

Alternatively, the mixture can be frozen in rigid containers, defrosted at room temperature for 2-3 hours, then put in a cake tin and baked.

Unbaked cake mixtures have a freezer life of 2 months.

Cheesecake

Cheesecake can be frozen baked or unbaked, although it should be frozen without cream or fruit toppings.

These can be added after defrosting.

Wrap a cheesecake in foil and overwrap in a plastic bag before freezing.

Cheesecake has a freezer life of 1 month. Defrost at room temperature for 4-6 hours.

Chocolate

Chocolate grates better for cooking if frozen first.

Chocolate has a freezer life of 2 months.

Choux pastry

Choux pastry can be frozen cooked or uncooked.

Uncooked pastry shapes should be open-frozen on non-stick baking trays before being packed into plastic bags.

Cooked pastry shapes should be open-frozen when cool and packed into rigid containers with layers of freezer wrap between the layers.

Choux pastry has a freezer life of 3 months if uncooked and 6 months if cooked.

Raw choux pastry should be cooked from frozen. Allow 5 minutes longer than the usual cooking time.

Cooked pastry shapes should be reheated in the oven for 10 minutes.

Christmas puddings

Traditional rich Christmas puddings keep very well and there is no point in freezing them.

However, if you make a lighter pudding it could be frozen. Boil it first for 6 hours, remove from the bowl when cold, wrap in greaseproof paper and foil, and freeze.

Christmas pudding has a freezer life of 4 months. It should be defrosted overnight.

To reheat, replace it in its original bowl, which has been well buttered, cover with buttered paper and foil, and boil for 2-3 hours.

Cold puddings

Mousses and cold soufflés freeze well. They should be decorated after defrosting and not before freezing.

Jellies do not freeze satisfactorily because they tend to weep on thawing and lose their bright appearance. They also become uneven and grainy.

However, gelatine used as a setting agent for mousses, cheesecake etc gives excellent results.

Cold puddings have a freezer life of 3 months and can be defrosted in the refrigerator in about 2 hours.

Croissants

Cooked croissants can be frozen in plastic bags or in rigid containers.

Unbaked croissant dough can also be frozen. Prepare to the stage where all the butter has been added but do not give the final rolling. Wrap in a plastic bag and freeze immediately.

Croissants have a freezer life of 3 months; unbaked dough, 6 weeks.

Baked croissants should be wrapped in foil straight from the freezer and placed in a moderate oven at 180°C for 15 minutes.

Loosen the wrappings of unbaked dough and refasten them, allowing room for the dough to rise, then thaw in the refrigerator overnight or at room temperature for 5 hours. Give the final rolling, shape and bake.

Crumpets

Crumpets can be frozen in plastic bags.

They have a freezer life of 6 months and can be toasted straight from the freezer of defrosted for 6 hours in their packaging.

Custard

Custard does not freeze satisfactorily. Egg custard, caramel custard and vanilla custard all separate during freezing.

Decorations

Cakes should be decorated after they have been thawed, just before serving. Otherwise, decorations such as nuts, cachous and grated chocolate may absorb moisture and change colour, affecting the appearance of the cake.

Glacé fruit, so expensive before Christmas, is usually discounted heavily in January so buy up big and freeze individual pieces in foil, then put the pieces into plastic bags. Thaw at room temperature for a couple of hours before using. It keeps for around 12 months.

Doughnuts

Ring doughnuts freeze better than jam doughnuts, which may become soggy.

Pack in plastic bags, expel the air and seal.

Filo pastry

Filo pastry may be frozen cooked or uncooked. Pack uncooked filo pastry into plastic bags, expel the air and seal.

Filo pastry has a freezer life of 2 months.

To defrost, allow it to stand at room temperature

for 2 hours or overnight in the refrigerator.

Fruit crumble

Make as usual and either freeze raw or freeze the crumble mixture separately.

Fruit crumbles have a freezer life of 3 months.

They can be cooked from frozen at 200°C for 1 hour if raw or reheated at 190°C for 30-40 minutes if cooked.

Fruit pies

Fruit pies may be frozen either before or after baking, although the crust is more tender and flaky when frozen before baking.

Use foil pie plates, rust-proof metal pie plates or heat-resistant pie plates.

Special treatment is needed to preserve the colour and flavour of some fruits used in unbaked pies.

Apple slices should be steamed for 2 minutes, cooled and drained, or dipped raw into a solution of $1/4$ teaspoon ascorbic acid to 1 cup water.

Peel peaches without scalding and slice. Mix peach slices or apricot halves with 1 tablespoon lemon juice or an ascorbic acid solution made by dissolving $1/8$ teaspoon ascorbic acid in 1 tablespoon water.

Coat berries or cherries with a mixture of sugar and plain flour (to thicken the juice).

See also Pastry, Pies

Fudge
Buttery fudge, chocolate, vanilla or butterscotch freeze well.

Ice cream
Ice cream freezes more quickly in a freezer than in a refrigerator and does not need stirring.

Ice cream should not be stored too long, whether homemade or purchased, because it becomes grainy.

Flavourings should be pure rather than synthetic. Fruit

purées are ideal and can, of course, be made when fruit is in season and frozen until required.

Allow ice cream to defrost a little before serving because it is too hard and lacks flavour if eaten straight from the freezer.

Commercial ice cream has a freezer life of 1 month and homemade ice cream and sorbets, 2 months.

Defrost in the refrigerator for 1 hour for a fruit and cream ice cream or 30 minutes for a sorbet.

Icing
If the cake is to be iced and decorated before freezing,

use only icing with a high fat content.

Glacé, boiled and icings containing beaten egg white dry out and crack after a short time in the freezer. Mock cream and whipped fresh cream freeze well.

Jellies *see* Cold puddings

Lamingtons and trifles
Freeze cake for lamingtons and trifles. It cuts into small squares neatly, and the icing or jelly sets very quickly, eliminating messy drips.

Marshmallows
Marshmallows keep indefinitely in a freezer without getting sticky or drying out — as long as the children don't know they're in there.

Meat pies
The fillings of meat pies must be cooked before freezing.

The pie can be baked or the filling added to unbaked pie shells to be baked later.

See also Pies *and* chapter 5, 'Meat'

Meringues
Make meringues in the usual way and when cool pack them into rigid containers and freeze. However, when frozen they are still very fragile, so

don't put anything on top of them.

Meringues have a freezer life of 3 months and will defrost in about 1 hour at room temperature.

A meringue cake, which consists of several round flat discs of meringue (about 25 cm across and 1 cm thick) cemented together with either whipped or flavoured butter cream between the layers, can be frozen and is an impressive dessert
You can assemble weeks ahead of a special occasion.

Thaw at room temperature for at least an hour.

Milk puddings

Rice puddings can be frozen but semolina is not worth freezing as it takes no longer to cook than to defrost and reheat.

Milk puddings have a freezer life of 3 months. Add a little milk and reheat in a pan over a low heat.

Mousses *see* Cold puddings

Muffins

Purchased muffins may be frozen in their original wrappings and over-wrapped in a plastic bag. Otherwise, wrap muffins in plastic, expel the air and seal.

Muffins have a freezer life of 6 months. They may be

toasted without being defrosted, or they may be defrosted for about 6 hours at room temperature.

Pancakes

Stack cooked pancakes with a piece of greaseproof paper between them. Wrap the whole stack in foil and freeze.

Pancakes have a freezer life of 2 months.

To defrost, unwrap, spread out and leave at room temperature for about 20 minutes, then use as required.

Alternatively, spread on a baking tray, loosely cover with foil and reheat for about 10 minutes in the oven at 200°C or in a lightly greased frying pan for about ½ minute on each side.

See also Batter

Pastry

Make shortcrust, puff or flaky pastry according to your usual recipe and freeze in convenient quantities.

Flaky and puff pastry should be prepared up to the last rolling. It's best to shape the pastry into a flat rectangle instead of leaving it in a ball as it will freeze and defrost faster.

Wrap each piece in foil or a plastic bag, overwrap several pieces in a plastic bag, seal and freeze.

Pastry can also be shaped into flan cases or tartlet cases and frozen, baked or unbaked, uncovered in their tins. When firm, remove and pack in plastic bags and stack into a box as the cases are rather fragile.

Pie lids can also be prepared and frozen. Cut out the pastry and stack with a piece of waxed paper between them. Place the pile on a piece of cardboard, wrap in foil, overwrap in a plastic bag and freeze.

The most practical way to store leftover pastry is to roll it out and line foil pie plates, then freeze them ready for filling and baking later.

Package the shells in rigid containers with well-fitting lids because they become very brittle in the freezer and need the extra protection.

Brushing the bottom pastry crust with butter before baking or, in the case of unbaked pies, before freezing will help prevent fillings from soaking into the pastry and making it soggy.

Pastry has a freezer life of 6 months if baked and 3 months if unbaked.

Unbaked pastry and pie lids should be defrosted at room temperature until soft enough to roll or shape.

Unbaked flan or tartlet cases should be returned to their original cases and baked from frozen, adding about 5 minutes to normal baking time.

Baked flan and tartlet cases should be defrosted at room temperature for about 1 hour and refreshed in the oven if required.

See also Filo pastry, Pies

Pies

Pies can be frozen baked or unbaked. Make double-crusted pies in patty tins and others in foil dishes.

If freezing unbaked do not make a steam vent. (Make the vent just before baking.) Open-freeze and, when hard, leave pies in foil dishes and seal with foil. Remove small pies from patty tins and pack in foil or plastic bags.

If freezing baked pies, underbake slightly as the pies will brown more when reheated. Cool quickly, pack in foil and freeze.

Pies or tarts with only a bottom crust can be filled and frozen very success-fully. They are better frozen before wrapping to avoid spoiling the surface of the filling during packing.

Unbaked pies have a freezer life of 3 months; baked meat pies, 3-4 months; and fruit pies, up to 6 months.

To defrost unbaked pies, unwrap and place in a preheated oven and bake as usual, allowing extra time. Cut a vent in the pastry when it begins to thaw.

Baked pies can be defrosted at room temperature for 2-4 hours, depending on the size of the pie, then reheated at 180°C.

Pizza
Cool the baked pizza and open-freeze, then wrap it in foil, overwrap with a plastic bag and return to the freezer.

Pizza has a recommended freezer life of 3 months.

It can be reheated from frozen at 200°C for about 35 minutes or defrosted for 2 hours at room temperature and reheated at 200°C for 15 minutes.

Puddings *see* Cold puddings, Milk puddings, Steamed puddings

Quiches
Quiches are best baked before being frozen.

After baking, open-freeze and when firm remove from the flan tin, wrap in foil, overwrap in a plastic bag, seal and freeze.

Quiches have a freezer life of 2 months.

Loosen the wrappings and defrost at room temperature for 2 hours to serve cold, or heat through at 180°C for about 20 minutes.

Rice pudding *see* Milk puddings

Sandwiches
Spread butter or margarine liberally on sandwiches to be frozen to prevent fillings seeping through.

As different sandwich fillings will keep for different lengths of time, it is best not to store any sandwiches in the freezer for longer than 1 month.

Sandwich fillings that freeze well include cream cheese with chopped dates, cheddar cheese and

chutney, peanut butter, corned beef and mustard, roast beef and horseradish, pork and apple sauce, ham, roast lamb and mint jelly, chicken, turkey, devon, mashed sardines, tuna and salmon.

Avoid fillings containing cooked egg whites, which become tough and dry with freezing.

Also avoid raw vegetables such as celery, lettuce, tomatoes and carrots, and salad cream or mayonnaise, which will curdle and separate.

You can flavour the butter with lemon juice, grated cheese, tomato paste, chopped herbs or whatever seems appropriate to the filling you choose.

When freezing school sandwiches in bulk, add each child's name to the sandwiches each likes.

This saves the horror of a child getting a loathed filling by mistake.

Pack sandwiches in groups of six or eight rather than individually. Place an extra slice of bread at the end of each package to help prevent them drying out.

Wrap sandwiches tightly in foil or pack into rigid containers. Thaw at room temperature for 2-4 hours.

Party sandwiches
Ribbon sandwiches are always a good standby at drinks parties and are useful to make ahead of time.

Use three slices of bread — alternating brown and white bread — to make the sandwiches. Press the uncut sandwiches under a weight, pack and freeze.

When needed, thaw a little, cut into 6 cm by 2 cm shapes, then complete the thawing process, garnish and serve.

Scones
Scones freeze very well if baked before freezing. Pack the cooked, cooled scones in plastic bags, seal and freeze.

Unbaked scone dough loses the ability to rise if frozen and the result after freezing and baking is flat and heavy.

Scones have a freezer life of 3 months.

Defrost them in their wrappings at room temperature for about 1 hour, or spread on a baking tray, cover with foil and reheat in the oven at 200°C for 10 minutes.

Semolina *see* Milk puddings

Shortbread
Shortbread stores well in an airtight tin for a week or two, but will keep much longer in the freezer and emerge in top condition. Make and bake in the usual way, cool and wrap in foil.

Shortbread has a freezer life of 3 months.

Defrost for about 4 hours at room temperature .

Sorbets
Both homemade and commercially prepared sorbets may be frozen. Whisk sorbet at intervals during the freezing process.

Sorbets have a freezer life of 2-3 months and must be allowed to soften before serving, so allow to sit at room temperature for about 10 minutes.

Soufflés

Soufflés freeze extremely well. Prepare the soufflé dish as usual but use foil rather than greaseproof paper to form the collar 3-4 cm above the rim of the dish. Secure it with freezer tape. Pour the mixture into the dish but do not decorate. Open-freeze until hard, then place the soufflé dish, with the collar still in position, in a plastic bag, seal and return to the freezer.

Soufflés have a recommended freezer life of 2 months.

To defrost soufflés to be served cold, remove the plastic bag (but not the collar) and defrost overnight in the refrigerator or at room temperature for about 4 hours.

When defrosted, carefully remove the collar and decorate the soufflé.

To serve hot, defrost small soufflés for 20 minutes at room temperature, large ones for 30 minutes, then bake at 190°C for 25-30 minutes (if in individual dishes) or 70 minutes (if in one large dish) until risen and golden.

Sponge cakes

Sponge cakes freeze beautifully and are always useful to have in the freezer. They should not be filled with jam or fruit before freezing as the filling will make the sponge go soggy when defrosted.

Either wrap the sponge layers separately or slip a piece of greaseproof paper between the layers before packing into a plastic bag or rigid container.

If the sponge is butter-iced, open-freeze before putting it in a plastic bag or rigid container and returning to the freezer.

Plain sponges have a freezer life of 4 months, butter-iced sponges, 3 months.

Defrost for about 2 hours at room temperature.

If the sponge is butter-iced, remove the wrappings first so that they don't stick to the surface.

See also Cakes, Icing

Steamed puddings

Both suet and sponge mixtures can be made and cooked in the usual way, then cooled, wrapped and frozen.

Dried fruits or chocolate can be added, but jam or syrup should not be placed in the bottom of the basin because it will make the pudding soggy when defrosting.

Steamed puddings have a freezer life of 3 months and can be reheated by boiling for 1 hour.

Vol-au-vent cases

Make vol-au-vent cases as usual, open-freeze them (unbaked) and, when hard, interleave them with pieces of moisture-proof paper and pack into plastic bags or rigid containers. Seal and return to the freezer.

Baked cases should be packed in rigid containers and labelled 'fragile'.

Vol-au-vent cases have a freezer life of 3 months if unbaked and 6 months if baked.

Raw cases can be baked direct from the freezer in a hot oven. Baked cases should be defrosted at room temperature for about 1 hour and reheated if desired for 5-10 minutes before filling.

Waffles

Bake waffles as usual and, when cold, pack in the required quantities in plastic bags or stack in rigid containers, seal and freeze.

Waffles have a freezer life of 2 months. Reheat from frozen under the grill or in the oven at 190°C for about 10 minutes until well browned.

Yeast

Divide fresh yeast into 15 or 30 g cubes, wrap each one in foil, put them all in a plastic bag and freeze.

Yeast has a freezer life of 1 month.

Defrost at room temperature for 30 minutes or put it straight into lukewarm water and activate as usual.

DAIRY PRODUCTS AND EGGS

Dairy foods are at their best when fresh. However, there are times when it is convenient and time- and money-saving to resort to freezer storage. For example, semi-prepared ingredients used a lot in cooking, such as whipped cream or roux for sauces, can be frozen.

Homogenised milk freezes reasonably well. It should never be frozen in milk bottles but it can be frozen in commercial milk cartons. Cream freezes well if the butterfat content is 35% or more. Cream with lower butterfat content separates on defrosting and should not be frozen. Whipped cream freezes very well. Butter may be frozen successfully in its commercial wrappings, although it needs to be overwrapped to prevent contamination by odours from other foods.

Prepared foods made from dairy products freeze very well indeed. Cheesecake and savoury butters are examples. (Ice cream is discussed in chapter 9, 'Desserts and baking'.)

Eggs freeze well if they are removed from their shells and separated. They can also be lightly beaten and then frozen in convenient portions in ice cube trays.

Blue cheese *see*
Cheese

Brandy butter

Cream together 250 g butter and 250 g icing sugar, then beat in about 6 tablespoons brandy, tasting as you go.

Pack in rigid containers in 125 g or 250 g quantities.

Brandy butter has a freezer life of 2 months.

Defrost at room temperature for 2-3 hours, then keep cool until required.

Butter

Unsalted butter freezes more successfully than salted butter.

Freeze butter made from pasteurised cream only. Butter made from unpasteurised cream will turn rancid rapidly and should never be frozen.

Because butter is easily affected by smells transferred from other foods, overwrap it with foil or plastic before freezing.

Divide butter into packages of a manageable size — about 500 g.

Both salted and unsalted butter have a freezer life of 6 months.

Defrost butter, unopened, in the refrigerator for 4$\frac{1}{2}$-5 hours.

Savoury butters are well worth having in the freezer

in readiness for entertaining. *See* Savoury butter.

Hard sauces such as rum butter or brandy butter can be frozen in plastic containers until required then defrosted in the refrigerator in about 2 hours. *See* Brandy butter.

Buttermilk

Buttermilk should be frozen in rigid containers or in the waxed cartons in which it is bought.

Buttermilk has a freezer life of 6 weeks.

Defrost buttermilk in its container overnight in the refrigerator. Whisk before using because it tends to separate when defrosted.

See also Milk

Cheese

Hard cheeses freeze very well, so it could be economical to buy a large cheese. Divide it into convenient portions and pack them in plastic bags. Expel surplus air. Cheese must be well wrapped to prevent transfer of flavours and drying out.

To defrost hard cheese, leave it in its wrapping in the refrigerator overnight.

Blue cheeses freeze well but crumble when thawed.

Cream cheese can be frozen only for about 6 weeks, but it can also be frozen as part of a prepared dish.

Grated cheese can be frozen in large quantities,

packed in plastic bags and used from frozen.

See also Cottage cheese, Curd cheese

Cottage cheese
Cottage cheese may be frozen if it is of good quality and made of pasteurised milk.

Place it in rigid containers for freezing, leaving some headspace.

Cottage cheese has a freezer life of 2-3 months.

Defrost at room temperature for 3½-4 hours.

Cream
Cream labelled 'thickened cream' usually has less than 35% butterfat content and freezes better as whipped cream. When frozen unwhipped, it separates on thawing and becomes grainy in texture.

'Rich cream' has a much higher butterfat content and will freeze equally well whipped or unwhipped.

Recipes often call for small amounts of cream, so it is worthwhile to fill ice cube trays with cream and freeze. When firm the tray should be overwrapped in a plastic bag.

One ice cube tray usually equals 1 tablespoon, but measure the sections of your ice cube tray to be sure.

See also Rosettes, Sour cream

Cream cheese *see*
Cheese

Curd cheese
Curd cheese does not freeze
satisfactorily unless it
contains more than 40%
butterfat.

Eggs
Do not freeze hard-boiled
eggs because the whites
develop a leathery texture
when frozen. Fresh eggs
freeze well but they must
be removed from their
shells.

Stir whole eggs lightly with
a fork to blend the white
and yolk, add 1/2 teaspoon
salt or sugar to every 6 eggs
to prevent thickening. Pack
into a waxed container and
label carefully.

Alternatively, the eggs can
be frozen in ice cube trays.
When frozen, transfer the
trays to plastic bags.

Mix egg yolks in the same
way and freeze in small
cartons or in ice cube trays.
One tablespoon of yolk
equals 1 egg yolk.

Egg whites can be frozen
without beating and with
no additions. Pack into
cartons or ice cube trays.
Two tablespoons of white
equals 1 egg white.

Eggs have a freezer life of 6
months and can be thawed
at room temperature for 40
minutes.

If egg whites are being used
for meringues they can be

broken up, thawed and beaten in one operation.

Goat's milk

Goat's milk has a freezer life of 1-3 months, depending on quality.

Grated cheese *see* Cheese

Ice cream *see* chapter 9, 'Desserts and baking'

Margarine

Cooking margarine can be frozen in the same way as butter.

Table margarine can be frozen in its own plastic container. Most brands will spread straight from the freezer, making defrosting unnecessary.

Milk

Pasteurised milk doesn't freeze well because the fat separates. Homogenised and skimmed milk will freeze but for only about a month.

Don't put a bottle of milk in the freezer because expansion will make it crack. Pour milk into a waxed or plastic container, allowing 2-3 cm headspace, seal and freeze. Commercial cartons of milk may be frozen without being repackaged.

Milk has a freezer life of 1 month. Defrost in the refrigerator overnight.

If milk is to be used for cooking it may be reheated gently from frozen.

See also Buttermilk, Goat's milk

Rosettes
When there is some cream left over after decorating a cake, pipe it out in rosettes, then freeze.

They can be used to float on top of cups of coffee on special occasions.

Roux
Roux for sauces can be made up using equal quantities of butter and flour, divided into 30 g/1 tablespoon portions, wrapped in foil and frozen.

Alternatively, the ice cube tray could be used as a container. One ice cube section equals about 1 tablespoon.

To make white sauce, drop 1 frozen roux pack into 250 ml milk and bring to the boil, stirring until thick and smooth.

Savoury butter
All types of savoury butter may be frozen.

Beat the butter and desired savoury flavourings together until well mixed, then place on freezer wrap and shape into a roll.

Roll the paper around the butter to cover it, then overwrap with a plastic bag.

Savoury butter has a freezer life of 3 months.

Defrost overnight in the refrigerator.

Sour cream

Sour cream freezes satisfactorily if it contains at least 35-40% butterfat and has a freezer life of 3 months.

Freeze it in its own carton or in rigid containers and defrost overnight in the refrigerator.

Yoghurt

Fruit-flavoured yoghurts tend to separate on defrosting but whipping will improve the texture. Yoghurt with honey freezes well.

Yoghurt has a freezer life of 1 month and can be defrosted overnight in the refrigerator.

F